INTERBEING

Other Books by Thich Nhat Hanh

INTERBEING

*Fourteen Guidelines
for Engaged Buddhism*

Third Edition

Thich Nhat Hanh

Edited by Fred Eppsteiner

Parallax Press
Berkeley, California

Parallax Press
P.O. Box 7355
Berkeley, CA 94707

© 1987, 1993, 1998 by Thich Nhat Hanh
Third edition 1998

All Rights Reserved
Printed in the United States of America
Design by Legacy Media, Inc.
Art and calligraphy by Kazuaki Tanahashi

LIBRARY OF CONGRESS CATALOGING-IN-PUBLICATION DATA

    Nhât Hanh, Thích.
        Interbeing: fourteen guidelines for engaged Buddhism /
    Thich Nhat Hanh. — 3rd ed. / edited by Fred Eppsteiner.
          p. cm.
        ISBN 1-888375-08-6 (pbk.)
        1. Tiep Hien (Religious Order) 2. Buddhist precepts.
    I. Eppsteiner, Fred. II. Title.
    BQ9800.T5293N4545   1997
    294.3'65—dc21   97-29779
                                         CIP

98 99 00 01 02 / 10 9 8 7 6 5 4 3 2

Contents

PART THREE
Ceremonies

PART FOUR
The Charter of the Order of Interbeing

Editor's Introduction

The Order of Interbeing *(Tiep Hien)* was formed by Thich Nhat Hanh in the mid-1960s, at a time when the Vietnam War was escalating and the teachings of the Buddha were desperately needed to combat the hatred, violence, and divisiveness enveloping his country. On the full moon day of February 1966, Zen Master Nhat Hanh ordained six members into the Order, three men and three women ranging in age from twenty-two to thirty-two. All of them were Board members of the School of Youth for Social Service, which he had helped found the year before.

From its inception, the Order of Interbeing was comprised of all four membership categories of the original Buddhist community *(Sangha)*—monks, nuns, laymen, and laywomen. Of the first six ordinees, the three women chose to live celibate lives like nuns, although they did not shave their heads or take all the formal vows of Buddhist nuns, and the three men chose to marry and practice as lay Buddhists.

The ordination was a wonderful celebration. Each ordinee was presented with a lamp with a handmade shade on which Thich Nhat Hanh had calligraphed Chinese characters like "Lamp of Wisdom," "Lamp of the Full Moon," and "Lamp of the World." During the ceremony, the six ordinees vowed to study, practice, and observe the Fourteen Mindfulness Trainings of the Order of Interbeing, a wonderful blend of traditional Buddhist morality and contemporary social concerns.

Forged in the crucible of war and devastation, these guidelines helped the first six brothers and sisters develop serenity and learn to look more deeply into things, even during the tragedy of war. Though they continued to stay busy helping war victims, organizing demonstrations, printing books and leaflets, running social service projects, and organizing an underground for draft resisters, they renewed themselves with a Day of Mindfulness each weekend. "I so looked forward to these days," recalls Sister Chân Không. "I dwelled mindfully on each act, beginning as I placed down my overnight bag in my room, boiled water to prepare a bath, and then put on my meditation clothes. First I did walking meditation alone in the woods and picked some wildflowers and bamboo branches for flower arrangements. Then, after a few hours of dwelling mindfully in each act and releasing most of my worries, I began to feel renewed." After practicing sitting and walking meditation, the six members gathered together to recite the Fourteen Mindfulness Trainings and chant the *Heart of the Prajñaparamita Sutra.*

For ten years, no new members were permitted to join the Order's core community. In fact, this "period of experimentation" was extended until 1981, when Anh Huong Nguyen, a microbiologist and lay meditation teacher, became the seventh member of the Order. Today, there are more than four hundred members of the core community and many thousands of others worldwide who recite the Fourteen Mindfulness Trainings regularly. The Order's journal, *The Mindfulness Bell,* lists hundreds of Sanghas around the globe, groups of people in local communities who come together to study, practice, and discuss the Fourteen Mindfulness Trainings.

In 1992, the Order of Interbeing held its first International Council. The second International Council, called "Being Wonderfully Together," was held in September 1996 and attended by more than one hundred core community members from four continents. An Executive Council was formed, and the Order's structure and activities were thoroughly reviewed. This third edition of the book *Interbeing* includes the newly updated Fourteen Mindfulness Trainings of the Order of Interbeing and the revised text of the Order's Charter. The Order is continuing to take shape as a true expression of the bodhisattva practice of socially engaged Buddhism.

The Fourteen Mindfulness Trainings of the Order of Interbeing remain uniquely applicable to contemporary moral dilemmas. The Order was formed at a time when destruction in the name of supposedly irreconcilable "isms" was painfully evident in Vietnam. Thich Nhat Hanh was acutely aware of the need for all people to overcome ideological divisiveness, and, accordingly, the first three trainings directly reject fanaticism and political or religious self-righteousness. The fourth goes to the heart of Buddhist compassion and directs a challenge to all practitioners: contemplative reflection on the suffering of living beings is not enough; we must help diminish suffering through compassionate involvement. This training suggests that the lotus flower grows most beautifully when planted deep in the mud.

The Fifth Mindfulness Training shows how Right Livelihood has implications beyond simply avoiding harmful professions; that the manner in which we spend our time, energy, and material resources is as much a moral concern as a practical one. The Sixth extends the traditional Buddhist precept concerning anger and directs us to apply an antidote as soon as anger arises, realizing that individual anger has far-reaching social effects. The Seventh Training, at the core of all fourteen, shows us how mindfulness, awareness, and returning to the breath are the keys to maintaining ourselves in the midst of activity.

The Eighth and Ninth Trainings address factionalism: communities rent by political, social, and religious division, issues as pressing today as in the war-torn environment in which they were forged. They provide a model of Right Speech and Right Action, never losing sight of the need to speak out about social injustice and oppression with the all-embracing, nonpartisan viewpoint of the Dharma. The traditional Buddhist admonition against killing is expanded in the Twelfth Mindfulness Training, which enjoins us not only to not destroy life, but to actively protect it. And does not the Thirteenth Training on non-stealing speak to the fact that the well-stocked shelves of one country relate directly to the empty shelves of another, that profit-making at the cost of human suffering and the suffering of other living beings is immoral?

The final Mindfulness Training deals with sexuality and reminds us that respecting life and committing ourselves to ending suffering is as real an issue within the most intimate area of human relationships as in the political and social arenas.

The Fourteen Mindfulness Trainings of the Order of Interbeing are guidelines for anyone wishing to live mindfully. By developing peace and serenity through ethical and conscientious living, we can help our society make the transition from one based on greed and consumerism to one in which thoughtfulness and compassionate action are of the deepest value. The Order of Interbeing makes real what is implicit in Buddhism and all the world's great religious traditions: that compassionate living, engaged in society, is most effective if based on the techniques for centering the self and the appreciation of the sacredness of all things great and small. The teachings and practice of Buddhism engaged in society can help us all.

Fred Eppsteiner
Naples, Florida
July 1997

PART ONE

The Order of Interbeing
(Tiep Hien)

The Order of Interbeing

THE MEANING OF *TIEP HIEN*

The word *tiep* means "being in touch with" and "continuing." *Hien* means "realizing" and "making it here and now." For us to better understand the spirit of the Tiep Hien Order, it is helpful to begin by examining these four expressions.

What are we to be in touch with? The answer is reality, the reality of the world and the reality of the mind. To be in touch with the mind means to be aware of the processes of our inner life—feelings, perceptions, mental formations—and also to rediscover our true mind, which is the wellspring of understanding and compassion. Getting in touch with true mind is like digging deep in the soil and reaching a hidden source that fills our well with fresh water. When we discover our true mind, we are filled with understanding and compassion, which nourishes us and those around us as well. Being in touch with the true mind is being in touch with *Buddhas* and *bodhisattvas*, enlightened beings who show us the way of understanding, peace, and happiness.

To be in touch with the reality of the world means to be in touch with everything that is around us in the animal, vegetal, and mineral realms. If we want to be in touch, we have to get out of our shell and look clearly and deeply at the wonders of life—the snowflakes, the moonlight, the beautiful flowers—and also the suffering—hunger, disease, torture, and oppression. Overflowing with understanding and compassion, we can appreciate the wonders of life, and, at the same time, act with the firm resolve to alleviate the suffering. Too many people distinguish between the inner world of our mind and the world outside, but these worlds are not separate. They belong to the same reality. The ideas of inside and outside are helpful in everyday life, but they can become an obstacle that prevents us from experiencing ultimate reality. If we look deeply into our mind, we see the world deeply at the same time. If we understand the world, we understand our mind. This is called "the unity of mind and world."

Modern Christianity uses the ideas of vertical and horizontal theology. Spiritual life is the vertical dimension of getting in touch with God, while social life is the horizontal dimension of getting in touch with humans. In Buddhism, there are people who also think in these terms. They speak about the higher level of practicing the Buddha's Way and the lower level of helping living beings. But this understanding does not accord with the true spirit of Buddhism, which teaches that Buddhahood, the nature of enlightenment, is innate to every being and not just a transcendental identity. Thus, in Buddhism the vertical and horizontal are one. If we penetrate the horizontal, we find the vertical, and vice versa. This is the meaning of "being in touch with."

Next we come to the concept of continuation. Tiep means to tie two strings together to make a longer string. It means extending and perpetuating the career of enlightenment that was started and nourished by the Buddhas and bodhisattvas who preceded us. It is helpful to remember that the word "Buddha" means a person who is awake. The word "bodhisattva" also signifies an enlightened person. The way of enlightenment that was started by the Buddhas and bodhisattvas should be continued, and this is the responsibility of all of us who undertake the practice of Buddhism. Sowing the seeds of enlightenment and taking good care of the tree of enlightenment are the meaning of tiep, "to continue."

The third concept is "to realize" or realization. Hien means not to dwell or be caught in the world of doctrines and ideas, but to bring and express our insights into real life. Ideas about understanding and compassion are not understanding and compassion. Understanding and compassion must be real in our lives. They must be seen and touched. The real presence of understanding and compassion will alleviate suffering and cause joy to be born. But to realize does not only mean to act. First of all, realization means transforming ourselves. This transformation creates a harmony between ourselves and nature, between our own joy and the joy of others. Once we get in touch with the source of understanding and compassion, this transformation is realized and all our actions will naturally protect and enhance life. If we wish to share joy and happiness with others, we must have joy and happiness within ourselves. If we wish to share calmness and serenity, we should first realize them within ourselves. Without a calm and peaceful mind, our actions will only create more trouble and destruction in the world.

The last expression to examine is "making it here and now." Only the present moment is real and available to us. The peace we desire is not in some distant future, but it is something we can realize in the present moment. To practice Buddhism does not mean to endure hardship now for the sake of peace and liberation in the future. The purpose of practice is not to be reborn in some paradise or Buddha-land after death. The purpose is to have peace for ourselves and others right now, while we are alive and breathing. Means and ends cannot be separated. Bodhisattvas are careful about causes, while ordinary people care more about effects, because bodhisattvas see that cause and effect are one. Means are ends in themselves. An enlightened person never says, "This is only a means." Based on the insight that means *are* ends, all activities and practices should be entered into mindfully and peacefully. While sitting, walking, cleaning, working, or serving, we should feel peace within ourselves. The aim of sitting meditation is first to be peaceful and awake during sitting meditation. Working to help the hungry or the sick means to be peaceful and loving during that work. When we practice, we do not expect the practice to pay large rewards in the future, even nirvana, the pure land, enlightenment, or Buddhahood. The secret of Buddhism is to be awake here and now. There is no way to peace; peace is the way. There is no way to enlightenment; enlightenment is the way. There is no way to liberation; liberation is the way.

Thus far, we have examined the meanings of the words "tiep" and "hien." In looking for an English word or phrase to express the meaning of Tiep Hien, the word "interbeing" has been proposed. It is a translation of a Chinese term found in the teaching of the *Avatamsaka Sutra*. I hope this recently invented word will be widely adopted in the near future.

2
MINDFULNESS TRAININGS

Members of the Order of Interbeing commit to observe and practice the Fourteen Mindfulness Trainings. In the sutras, the Buddha often used the word *shila* (precepts) to describe these trainings, but he also used the word *siksha* (trainings). This latter term is more consistent with the Buddhist understanding of how to practice these guidelines, and so I have recently begun using "mindfulness trainings" instead of "precepts."

Mindfulness trainings are practices, not prohibitions. They do not restrict our freedom. They protect us, guarantee our liberty, and prevent us from getting entangled in difficulties and confusion. When we fail, we lift ourselves up and try again to do our best. In fact, we can never succeed one hundred percent. The mindfulness trainings are like the North Star. If we want to travel north, we can use the North Star to guide us, but we never expect to arrive at the North Star.

Mindfulness trainings should be understood and practiced in terms of the Threefold Training: mindfulness, concentration, and insight. Mindfulness leads to concentration, and concentration leads to insight. The Fourteen Mindfulness Trainings are a concrete expression of mindfulness in daily life.

3
THE CHARTER OF THE ORDER OF INTERBEING

According to the Charter of the Order of Interbeing, "The aim of the Order is to actualize Buddhism by studying, experimenting with, and applying Buddhism in modern life." Understanding can only be attained through direct experience. The results of the practice should be tangible and verifiable.

The Charter lists four principles as the foundation of the Order: nonattachment from views, direct experimentation on the nature of interdependent origination through meditation, appropriateness, and skillful means. Let us examine each of these principles.

1. Nonattachment from views: To be attached means to be caught in dogmas, prejudices, habits, and what we consider to be the Truth. The first aim of the practice is to be free of all attachments, especially attachments to views. This is the most important teaching of Buddhism.

2. Direct experimentation: Buddhism emphasizes the direct experience of reality, not speculative philosophy. Direct practice-realization, not intellectual research, brings about insight. Our own life is the instrument through which we experiment with truth.

3. Appropriateness: A teaching, in order to bring about understanding and compassion, must reflect the needs of people and the realities of society. To do this, it must meet two criteria: it must conform with the basic tenets of Buddhism, and it must be truly helpful and relevant. It is said that there are 84,000 Dharma doors through which one can enter Buddhism. For Buddhism to continue as a living source of wisdom and peace, even more doors should be opened.

4. Skillful means (upaya): Skillful means consist of images and methods created by intelligent teachers to show the Buddha's Way and guide people in their efforts to practice the Way in their own particular circumstances. These means are called Dharma doors.

Concerning these four principles, the Charter says, "The spirit of nonattachment from views and the spirit of direct experimentation lead to open-mindedness and compassion, both in the realm of the perception of reality and in the realm of human relationships. The spirit of appropriateness and the spirit of skillful means lead to a capacity to be creative and to reconcile, both of which are necessary for the service of living beings." Guided by these principles, the Order of Interbeing has an open attitude towards all Buddhist schools. The Order of Interbeing does not consider any sutra or group of sutras as its basic text. Inspiration is drawn from the essence of the Buddhadharma as found in all sutras. The Order does not recognize any systematic arrangement of the Buddhist teachings as proposed by various schools of Buddhism. The Order seeks to realize the Dharma spirit within early Buddhism as well as the development of that spirit throughout the Sangha's history and the teachings in all Buddhist traditions.

In addition, the Charter expresses a willingness to be open and to change. "The Order of Interbeing rejects dogmatism in both looking and acting. It seeks all forms of action that can revive and sustain the true spirit of insight and compassion in life. It considers this spirit to be more important than any Buddhist institution or tradition. With the aspiration of a bodhisattva, members of the Order of Interbeing seek to change themselves in order to change society in the direction of compassion and understanding by living a joyful and mindful life."

4

THE COMMUNITY

The Order of Interbeing consists of a core community and an extended community. The core community is composed of members who have made the commitment to practice the Fourteen Mindfulness Trainings of the Order. The extended community consists of those who attempt to live up to the spirit of the Order, but who have not formally made this commitment. Members of the extended community cooperate closely with core community members in all activities, including the recitation of the Fourteen Mindfulness Trainings. To become a member of the core community, a person undergoes a one-year apprenticeship, practicing with members of a core community. After joining the core community, he or she agrees to observe at least sixty days of mindfulness a year.

5

THE MINDFULNESS TRAININGS
OF THE ORDER OF INTERBEING

Buddhist mindfulness trainings are guidelines for everyday living. Most religious rules are prohibitions that begin with the control of bodily actions—not to kill, steal, and so forth. The Fourteen Mindfulness Trainings of the Order of Interbeing begin with the mind, and the first seven deal with problems associated with the mind. According to the Buddha, "The mind is the king of all dharmas. The mind is the painter who paints everything." The Fourteen Mindfulness Trainings reflect the Eightfold Path, the basic teaching of both Theravada and Mahayana Buddhism.[1] The Eightfold

---

[1]   See Thich Nhat Hanh, *The Heart of the Buddha's Teaching* (Berkeley: Parallax Press, 1997).

Path can be described as the essential training. The Eightfold Path also begins with the mind—Right View and Right Thought. We can arrange the Fourteen Trainings into three categories. The first seven deal with the mind, the next two with speech, and the last five with the body, although we must realize that this division is arbitrary. The mind is like a lamp of awareness, always present. Those who regularly recite and practice the mindfulness trainings will see this.

6
RECITING THE MINDFULNESS TRAININGS

The Fourteen Mindfulness Trainings are recited at least once every two weeks. Usually, a member of the core community is asked to lead the recitation. However, a member of the extended community can also be invited to lead. Participants sit in two rows facing each other. The person who sits at the beginning of the row on the right, nearest the altar, is called the "head of the ceremony." He or she leads the ceremony and is responsible for inviting the bell to sound. The person who sits directly opposite him or her recites the trainings. The recitation should be neither too slow nor too quick, as the right speed will please the community. The leader of the recitation should be visible to everyone.

At the beginning of the recitation is the Sanghakarman Procedure, in which it is confirmed that there is harmony in the Community, that everyone is present, and that today is the proper date for reciting the Fourteen Mindfulness Trainings. Then, the head of the ceremony offers incense and recites aloud the incense-offering verse. The rest of the community stands up and, with palms joined, follows their breathing. After the incense offering, the head of the ceremony invokes the names of Shakyamuni, Manjushri, Samantabhadra, Avalokiteshvara, Maitreya, and all ancestral teachers. After each name is invoked, everyone bows together. Then the members of the community sit down. When everyone is completely settled, the bell is invited to sound, and the recitation begins with the sutra-opening verse. From the very beginning of the ceremony and recitation, everyone follows his or her breathing and practices mindfulness in each movement. When listening, joining palms together, bowing, sitting down, or even adjusting posture, there is an appropriate verse for each movement.[2]

During the recitation, each member of the community should give full attention to the mindfulness training being read in order to receive and examine its content. Concentrating on the trainings this way will keep distracting thoughts from the mind. The person who recites them should speak in a clear voice that communicates the spirit of the trainings. The community's successful concentration depends on the quality of her recitation.

She begins by asking, "Brothers and Sisters, are you ready?" and each person answers silently, "I am ready." After reciting each training, she should pause for the length of three breaths, in and out, before asking, "This is the (First) Mindfulness Training of the Order of Interbeing. Have you studied, practiced, and observed it during the past two weeks?" This pause allows everyone to dwell on the essence and the content of the training. The answer to the question

---

[2] See *Plum Village Chanting and Recitation Book* (Berkeley: Parallax Press, 1997) for incense offering verse, invoking the bodhisattvas' names, and verses for various movements. See also Thich Nhat Hanh, *Present Moment Wonderful Moment: Mindfulness Verses for Daily Living* (Berkeley: Parallax Press, 1989).

falls somewhere between yes and no. Everyone who practices mindfulness and follows the trainings is entitled to say yes; it would be wrong to say no. But our yes is not absolutely firm, because our efforts during the past two weeks may not have been enough. So our answer is something like, "Yes, but I could have done better." We should allow time for the question to go deep into our mind and heart and act on us during the silence of the three breaths. While allowing the question to enter us, we can follow our breathing attentively. The head of ceremony should deeply observe three breaths before inviting the bell to sound, and the reciter should maintain awareness of the community's questioning. When the bell sounds, the entire community joins their palms, and the person reciting proceeds to the next mindfulness training. During this time of breathing, if anyone has a copy of the text of the ceremony, he or she should refrain from touching the page until the bell sounds. Practicing in this way creates a serene atmosphere.

PART TWO

Commentaries on the
Fourteen Mindfulness Trainings

The Fourteen Mindfulness Trainings

1

Aware of the suffering created by fanaticism and intolerance, we are determined not to be idolatrous about or bound to any doctrine, theory, or ideology, even Buddhist ones. Buddhist teachings are guiding means to help us learn to look deeply and to develop our understanding and compassion. They are not doctrines to fight, kill, or die for.

2

Aware of the suffering created by attachment to views and wrong perceptions, we are determined to avoid being narrow-minded and bound to present views. We shall learn and practice nonattachment from views in order to be open to others' insights and experiences. We are aware that the knowledge we presently possess is not changeless, absolute truth. Truth is found in life, and we will observe life within and around us in every moment, ready to learn throughout our lives.

3

Aware of the suffering brought about when we impose our views on others, we are committed not to force others, even our children, by any means whatsoever—such as authority, threat, money, propaganda, or indoctrination—to adopt our views. We will respect the right of others to be different and to choose what to believe and how to decide. We will, however, help others renounce fanaticism and narrowness through compassionate dialogue.

4

Aware that looking deeply at the nature of suffering can help us develop compassion and find ways out of suffering, we are determined not to avoid or close our eyes before suffering. We are committed to finding ways, including personal contact, images, and sounds, to be with those who suffer, so we can understand their situation deeply and help them transform their suffering into compassion, peace, and joy.

5

Aware that true happiness is rooted in peace, solidity, freedom, and compassion, and not in wealth or fame, we are determined not to take as the aim of our life fame, profit, wealth, or sensual pleasure, nor to accumulate wealth while millions are hungry and dying. We are committed to living simply and sharing our time, energy, and material resources with those in need. We will practice mindful consuming, not using alcohol, drugs, or any other products that bring toxins into our own and the collective body and consciousness.

6

Aware that anger blocks communication and creates suffering, we are determined to take care of the energy of anger when it arises and to recognize and transform the seeds of anger that lie deep in our consciousness. When anger comes up, we are determined not to do or say anything, but to practice mindful breathing or mindful walking and acknowledge, embrace, and look deeply into our anger. We will learn to look with the eyes of compassion at those we think are the cause of our anger.

7

Aware that life is available only in the present moment and that it is possible to live happily in the here and now, we are committed to training ourselves to live deeply each moment of daily life. We will try not to lose ourselves in dispersion or be carried away by regrets about the past, worries about the future, or craving, anger, or jealousy in the present. We will practice mindful breathing to come back to what is happening in the present moment. We are determined to learn the art of mindful living by touching the wondrous, refreshing, and healing elements that are inside and around us, and by nourishing seeds of joy, peace, love, and understanding in ourselves, thus facilitating the work of transformation and healing in our consciousness.

8

Aware that the lack of communication always brings separation and suffering, we are committed to training ourselves in the practice of compassionate listening and loving speech. We will learn to listen deeply without judging or reacting and refrain from uttering words that can create discord or cause the community to break. We will make every effort to keep communications open and to reconcile and resolve all conflicts, however small.

9

Aware that words can create suffering or happiness, we are committed to learning to speak truthfully and constructively, using only words that inspire hope and confidence. We are determined not to say untruthful things for the sake of personal interest or to impress people, nor to utter words that might cause division or hatred. We will not spread news that we do not know to be certain nor criticize or condemn things of which we are not sure. We will do our best to speak out about situations of injustice, even when doing so may threaten our safety.

10

Aware that the essence and aim of a Sangha is the practice of understanding and compassion, we are determined not to use the Buddhist community for personal gain or profit or transform our community into a political instrument. A spiritual community should, however, take a clear stand against oppression and injustice and should strive to change the situation without engaging in partisan conflicts.

11

Aware that great violence and injustice have been done to our environment and society, we are committed not to live with a vocation that is harmful to humans and nature. We will do our best to select a livelihood that helps realize our ideal of understanding and compassion. Aware of global economic, political and social realities, we will behave responsibly as consumers and as citizens, not investing in companies that deprive others of their chance to live.

12

Aware that much suffering is caused by war and conflict, we are determined to cultivate nonviolence, understanding, and compassion in our daily lives, to promote peace education, mindful mediation, and reconciliation within families, communities, nations, and in the world. We are determined not to kill and not to let others kill. We will diligently practice deep looking with our Sangha to discover better ways to protect life and prevent war.

13

Aware of the suffering caused by exploitation, social injustice, stealing, and oppression, we are committed to cultivating loving kindness and learning ways to work for the well-being of people, animals, plants, and minerals. We will practice generosity by sharing our time, energy, and material resources with those who are in need. We are determined not to steal and not to possess anything that should belong to others. We will respect the property of others, but will try to prevent others from profiting from human suffering or the suffering of other beings.

14

(For lay members): Aware that sexual relations motivated by craving cannot dissipate the feeling of loneliness but will create more suffering, frustration, and isolation, we are determined not to engage in sexual relations without mutual understanding, love, and a long-term commitment. In sexual relations, we must be aware of future suffering that may be caused. We know that to preserve the happiness of ourselves and others, we must respect the rights and commitments of

ourselves and others. We will do everything in our power to protect children from sexual abuse and to protect couples and families from being broken by sexual misconduct. We will treat our bodies with respect and preserve our vital energies (sexual, breath, spirit) for the realization of our bodhisattva ideal. We will be fully aware of the responsibility of bringing new lives into the world, and will meditate on the world into which we are bringing new beings.

(For monastic members): Aware that the aspiration of a monk or a nun can only be realized when he or she wholly leaves behind the bonds of worldly love, we are committed to practicing chastity and to helping others protect themselves. We are aware that loneliness and suffering cannot be alleviated by the coming together of two bodies in a sexual relationship, but by the practice of true understanding and compassion. We know that a sexual relationship will destroy our life as a monk or a nun, will prevent us from realizing our ideal of serving living beings, and will harm others. We are determined not to suppress or mistreat our body or to look upon our body as only an instrument, but to learn to handle our body with respect. We are determined to preserve vital energies (sexual, breath, spirit) for the realization of our bodhisattva ideal.

THE FIRST MINDFULNESS TRAINING
OPENNESS

Aware of the suffering created by fanaticism and intolerance, we are determined not to be idolatrous about or bound to any doctrine, theory, or ideology, even Buddhist ones. Buddhist teachings are guiding means to help us learn to look deeply and to develop our understanding and compassion. They are not doctrines to fight, kill, or die for.

వా

When we read sutras, discourses of the Buddha, we often hear the expression, "the great roar of the lion." This means the truth loudly and clearly proclaimed by the Buddha himself or one of his great disciples. The First Mindfulness Training of the Order of Interbeing is very much in that tradition. It is the compassionate voice of the Buddha calling to us.

The Buddha regarded his own teachings as a raft to cross the river and not as an absolute truth to be worshiped or clung to. He said this to prevent rigid dogmatism or fanaticism from taking root. Ideological inflexibility is responsible for so much of the conflict and violence in the world. Many Buddhist texts, including the *Kalama, Arittha (Knowing the Better Way to Catch a Snake),* and *Vajracchedika (Diamond That Cuts through Illusion)* sutras, address this important subject. According to Buddhist teachings, knowledge itself can be an obstacle to true understanding, and views can be a barrier to insight. Clinging to views can prevent us from arriving at a deeper, more profound understanding of reality. Buddhism urges us to transcend even our own knowledge if we wish to advance on the Path of Awakening. Views (*drishti*) are regarded as "obstacles to knowledge."

The First Mindfulness Training of the Order of Interbeing opens us to the total openness and absolute tolerance of Buddhism. Openness and tolerance are not merely ways to deal with people in daily life; they are truly gateways for the realization of the Way. According to Buddhism, if we do not continue to expand the boundaries of our understanding, we will be imprisoned by our views and unable to realize the Way.

In the *Sutra of One Hundred Parables,* the Buddha tells the story of a young merchant and his son. The merchant, a widower, loved his son dearly, but lost him due to the lack of wisdom. One day, while the man was away, his little boy was kidnapped by a gang of bandits, who razed the entire village before fleeing. When the young merchant returned home, he found the charred remains of a child near where his house had been, and in his suffering and confusion, mistook the charred remains for his own son. He cried unceasingly, arranged a cremation ceremony, and then carried the bag of ashes with him day and night, tied around his neck. A few months later, his little boy was able to escape from the bandits and find his way home. At midnight, he knocked on the door of his father's rebuilt house, but the father, thinking that some mischievous boy was ridiculing him, refused to open the door. The boy knocked and knocked, but the merchant clung to his view that his boy was dead, and eventually his son had to go away. This father who loved too much lost his son forever.

The Buddha said that when we are attached to views, even if the truth comes to our house and knocks on our door, we

will refuse to let it in. To inflexibly embrace a view and re-
gard it as fixed truth is to end the vital process of inquiry and
awakening. The Buddha's teachings are a *means* of helping
people. They are not an *end* to worship or fight over.

Clinging fanatically to an ideology or a doctrine not only
prevents us from learning, but also creates bloody conflicts.
The worst enemies of Buddhism are fanaticism and narrowness. Religious and ideological wars have marred the land-
scape of human history for millennia. Holy wars do not have
a place in Buddhism, because killing destroys the value of
Buddhism itself. The destruction of lives and moral values
during the Vietnam War was very much the fruit of fanaticism and narrowness. The Order of Interbeing was born
during that situation of utmost suffering, like a lotus flower
arising from a sea of fire. Understood in this context, the
First Mindfulness Training of the Order of Interbeing is the
compassionate voice of the Buddha in an ocean of hatred
and violence.

The First Mindfulness Training includes all the others, including the training not to kill but to protect all life. According to Buddhism, actions arise in three domains: body,
speech, and mind. We usually think that killing occurs in the
domain of the body, but a fanatical mind can cause the
killing of not just one, but millions of human beings. If we
follow the guidance of the First Mindfulness Training, all
weapons become useless.

If various kinds of medicine are needed to treat a variety
of diseases, Buddhism also needs to propose various Dharma doors for people of differing circumstances. While these
Dharma doors may differ from one another, they are all
Dharma doors. In the same way, distinct ailments are treated

with particular medicines, but all treatments use some kind of medicine, even if the medicine is merely water, air, or massage. The teachings and practices found in Buddhism may vary, but they all aim at liberating the mind. The Buddha said, "The water in the four oceans has only one taste, the taste of emancipation." Students of Buddhism need to view the various teachings in the same light. Openness and nonattachment from views should be guiding principles for all endeavors towards reconciliation and peace. They are also the doors leading into the world of ultimate reality and absolute freedom.

THE SECOND MINDFULNESS TRAINING
NONATTACHMENT FROM VIEWS

Aware of the suffering created by attachment to views and wrong perceptions, we are determined to avoid being narrow-minded and bound to present views. We shall learn and practice nonattachment from views in order to be open to others' insights and experiences. We are aware that the knowledge we presently possess is not changeless, absolute truth. Truth is found in life, and we will observe life within and around us in every moment, ready to learn throughout our lives.

৯৯

The Second Mindfulness Training is born from the First, and deals with the mind also. This training warns us not to get caught in our own knowledge. Knowledge may be necessary to think and to judge, and may be helpful in many parts of our daily life, but it is not the highest truth. When we contemplate a sunset, we think that the sun is above the horizon, but a scientist will tell us that the sun already set eight minutes earlier. It takes that long for us to see it. We realize that we saw only the sun of the past and not the sun of the present, that our perception was erroneous. But if we were to cling to our previous knowledge, we would lose the opportunity to advance in our understanding.

Buddhism teaches us to look at things in their nature of interbeing and dependent co-arising. When we do this, we free ourselves from a world in which each thing appears to have an individual identity. The mind that sees things in their interbeing, dependent co-arising nature is called the mind of nondiscriminative understanding. This mind transcends all views. In Zen Buddhism, there is an expression describing this state of insight: "The road of speech has been blocked, the path of the mind has been cut."

"Truth is found in life" and not merely in conceptual knowledge. How do we practice this? By observing reality in ourselves and in the world at all times. This is the Buddhist answer. To continually observe life is to practice according to the method of the *Sutra on the Four Establishments of Mindfulness (Satipatthana)*. The sutra teaches us how to be aware of what is going on in our body, our feelings, our mind, and the object of our mind, which is the world. The practice of mindfulness can help us develop concentration and insight, so that we can see reality as it is.

THE THIRD MINDFULNESS TRAINING
FREEDOM OF THOUGHT

Aware of the suffering brought about when we impose our views on others, we are committed not to force others, even our children, by any means whatsoever—such as authority, threat, money, propaganda, or indoctrination—to adopt our views. We will respect the right of others to be different and to choose what to believe and how to decide. We will, however, help others renounce fanaticism and narrowness through compassionate dialogue.

৪৯

This Third Mindfulness Training deals with the issue of freedom of thought, and therefore with the mind. Many parents, without being aware of it, do not follow this mindfulness training. Respecting other peoples' viewpoints is a hallmark feature of Buddhism. The *Kalama Sutta* is one of the earliest charters for free inquiry. In it, the Buddha discusses the problem of who or what to believe in and which doctrine is the best. The Buddha says, "It is fine to have doubt. Do not believe in something just because people think highly of it, or because it has come from tradition, or because it is found in scriptures. Consider whether it goes against your judgment, whether it could cause harm, whether it is condemned by wise people, and, above all, whether put into practice it will bring about destruction and pain. Anything that you judge to be beautiful, accords with your judgment, is appreciated by wise people, and, once put into practice, will bring about joy and happiness, can be accepted and put into practice."

As a shadow follows an object, the Third Mindfulness Training follows the Second, because the attitude of openness and nonattachment from views creates respect for the freedom of others. Freedom is one of the most basic rights of human beings—of all humans and not just some. To be able to respect others' freedom, we need to free ourselves from attachment and fanaticism and help others to do the same. How can we help other people? "Through compassionate dialogue," says this training. Compassionate dialogue is the essence of nonviolent action *(ahimsa)*. Ahimsa begins with the energy of tolerance and loving kindness, which will be expressed in gentle, compassionate, intelligent speech that can move people's hearts. It then moves into the field of action to create moral and social pressure for people to change. Understanding and compassion must be the basis of all nonviolent actions. Actions motivated by anger or hatred cannot be described as nonviolent.

As parents, we must respect freedom of thought in our children, even if they are still very young. This will allow us to learn from our children. Each human being is unique in his or her characteristics, capacities, and preferences. We should try to be open in order to see and understand our children and refrain from merely imposing our predispositions on them. Although blossoms also belong to the tree, they are not the same as the roots, leaves, and twigs. We should allow blossoms to be blossoms, leaves to be leaves, and twigs to be twigs, so that each can realize its highest capacity for development.

THE FOURTH MINDFULNESS TRAINING
AWARENESS OF SUFFERING

Aware that looking deeply at the nature of suffering can help us develop compassion and find ways out of suffering, we are determined not to avoid or close our eyes before suffering. We are committed to finding ways, including personal contact, images, and sounds, to be with those who suffer, so we can understand their situation deeply and help them transform their suffering into compassion, peace, and joy.

༄

The first Dharma talk given by the Buddha was on the Four Noble Truths. This First Truth is *dukkha*, the presence of suffering. This is the starting point of all Buddhist practice. If we are not aware that we are unwell, we will not know how to seek treatment, and we cannot be healed. The Second Truth is the cause of suffering, the Third is the possibility of removing it, and the Fourth tells us how to do it. These are liberating truths. But we cannot seek for the other three if we do not accept the presence of the first.

Suffering can have a therapeutic power. It can help us open our eyes. Awareness of suffering encourages us to search for its cause, to find out what is going on within us and in society. But we have to be careful. Too much suffering can destroy our capacity to love. We have to know our limits, to stay in touch with things that are dreadful in life and also things that are wonderful. If the First Truth explains the presence of suffering in life, the Third Truth encourages us to touch life's joy and peace. When people say that Buddhism is pessimistic, it is because they are stressing the First Truth and overlooking the Third. Mahayana Buddhism takes great care to emphasize the Third Truth. Its literature is full of references to the green willow, the violet bamboo, and the full moon as manifestations of the true Dharma.

Interconnections between other beings and ourselves are intimate. When we are peaceful and happy, we will not create suffering in others. When we work to alleviate the suffering in others, we feel peaceful and happy. Practice is not just for ourselves, but for others and the whole of society. The meaning of *mahayana*, the great vehicle, is to help ourselves and others, to liberate ourselves *and* others.

Teachers who say not to pay attention to the problems of the world like hunger, war, oppression, and social injustice, who say that we should only practice, have not understood deeply enough the meaning of mahayana. Of course, we should practice counting the breath, meditation, and sutra study, but what is the purpose of doing these things? It is to be aware of what is going on in ourselves and in the world. What is going on in the world is also going on within ourselves, and vice versa. Once we see this clearly, we will not refuse to take a position or to act. When a village is being bombed and children and adults are suffering from wounds and death, can a Buddhist sit still in his unbombed temple? If he has wisdom and compassion, he will find ways to practice Buddhism *while* helping other people. To practice Buddhism, it is said, is to see into one's own nature and become a Buddha. If we cannot see what is going on around us, how can we see into our own nature? There is a relationship between the nature of the self and the nature of suffering, injustice, and war. To see into the true nature of the world's weapons is to see into our own true nature.

Staying in touch with the reality of suffering keeps us sane and nourishes the wellsprings of understanding *(prajña)* and compassion *(karuna)* in us. It affirms in us the will to practice the bodhisattva's way: "Living beings are numberless; I vow to help by rowing them to the other shore." If we cut ourselves off from the reality of suffering, this vow will have no meaning. When we help children see and understand the suffering of humans and other living beings, we nourish compassion and understanding in them. Every act—even eating a sandwich or spending money—is an occasion for us to practice awareness. We must practice in each moment of daily life and not just in the meditation hall.

THE FIFTH MINDFULNESS TRAINING
SIMPLE, HEALTHY LIVING

Aware that true happiness is rooted in peace, solidity, freedom, and compassion, and not in wealth or fame, we are determined not to take as the aim of our life fame, profit, wealth, or sensual pleasure, nor to accumulate wealth while millions are hungry and dying. We are committed to living simply and sharing our time, energy, and material resources with those in need. We will practice mindful consuming, not using alcohol, drugs, or any other products that bring toxins into our own and the collective body and consciousness.

ॐ

Like a branch growing out from the trunk of a tree, the Fifth Mindfulness Training emerges naturally from the Fourth. The aim of Buddhist life is to realize insight (prajña) and to help people *(maitrya)*, and not to gain fame, power, or wealth. How can we have time to live the Buddhist ideal if we are constantly pursuing wealth or fame? If we do not live simply, we have to work all the time to pay our bills, and there is little time left for practice. The *Sutra on the Eight Realizations of the Great Beings* says, "The human mind is always searching for possessions and never feels fulfilled. This causes impure actions ever to increase. Bodhisattvas, however, always remember the principle of having few desires. They live a simple life in peace in order to practice the Way, and consider the realization of perfect understanding as their only career."[1]

In the context of modern society, simple living also means to remain as free as possible from the destructive momentum of social and economic pressures, to avoid modern diseases such as stress, depression, high blood pressure, and heart disease. We must resolve to oppose the type of modern life filled with pressures and anxieties that so many people now live. The only way out is to consume less, to be content with fewer possessions. We must discuss this with others who share our concern for finding better ways to live simply and happily together. Once we are able to live simply and happily, we are better able to help others. We have more time and energy to share. Sharing is difficult if you are wealthy. Bodhisattvas who practice the *paramita* of living a simple life are able to give both their time and their energy to others.

THE SIXTH MINDFULNESS TRAINING
DEALING WITH ANGER

Aware that anger blocks communication and creates suffering, we are determined to take care of the energy of anger when it arises and to recognize and transform the seeds of anger that lie deep in our consciousness. When anger comes up, we are determined not to do or say anything, but to practice mindful breathing or mindful walking and acknowledge, embrace, and look deeply into our anger. We will learn to look with the eyes of compassion at those we think are the cause of our anger.

---

[1] Thich Nhat Hanh, trans., *The Sutra on the Eight Realizations of the Great Beings* (Berkeley: Parallax Press, 1987), p. 4.

ℬ

When anger or hatred arises, we need to prepare the ground so that understanding can arise. If we stop thinking, speaking, and acting, the space for us to see and understand will open up. So the moment we feel irritation arising, we need to breathe in and out consciously, putting the whole of our mind into our breathing. Then, with the energy of mindfulness, we can look deeply and see how the person who is making us angry may have helped us in the past, or how that person has suffered, or how we ourselves have been unskillful. It may take just a few moments for us to realize this, or it may take several days. Until we come to some understanding, it is best if we refrain from saying anything to the person towards whom we feel anger. Practicing walking meditation and conscious breathing is enough.

When we grow a lemon tree, we want it to be vigorous and beautiful. But if it isn't vigorous and beautiful, we don't blame the tree. We observe it in order to understand why it isn't growing well. Perhaps we have not taken good care of it. We know it is funny to blame a lemon tree, but we do blame human beings when they are not growing well. Because our brothers, sisters, and children are humans, we think they should behave in certain ways. But human beings are not very different from lemon trees. If we take good care of them, they will grow properly. Blaming never helps. Only love and understanding can help people change. If we take good care of people, we will be rewarded by their pleasantness. Is this much different from the rewards we receive from our lemon tree?

If I had been born in the social conditions of a pirate and raised as a pirate, I would be a pirate now. A variety of interdependent causes has created the existence of the pirate. The responsibility is not solely his or his family's, but it is also society's. As I write these lines, hundreds of babies are being born near the Gulf of Siam. If politicians, educators, economists, and others do not do something to prevent it, many of these babies will become pirates in twenty-five years. Each of us shares some responsibility for the presence of pirates. Meditating on dependent origination and looking with compassionate eyes helps us see our duty and responsibility to suffering beings. Due to his capacity of seeing, the Bodhisattva Avalokiteshvara is capable of loving and acting. The purpose of meditation is to see and to hear.

"Seeds of anger that lie deep in our consciousness" means that the anger or hatred has not manifested. This mindfulness training advises us to use preventative medicine. We might think it is impossible to transform unconscious anger and hatred, that the time to transform them is when we are already feeling angry. But we *can* transform anger and hatred before they arise. During sitting meditation, we can shine the light of awareness on our unpleasant feelings and thus identify their roots. We can look directly at feelings we usually prefer to avoid, and just by our looking at them they will begin to transform. Then, when they rise up from our subconscious in the form of anger, they will not take us by surprise. Or we can plant seeds of love, compassion, and understanding in our daily lives, and those seeds will weaken the seeds of our anger. We do not have to wait for the anger to arise to do this work. In fact, it will be much more difficult to do it once anger has already arisen.

It may happen that we feel joyful and peaceful for one or two weeks, but this does not mean that during that time the seeds of anger are not there in our store consciousness. For example, when someone says something that hurts us, we may not react right away. But several weeks later, we might become angry at that person for some very small reason.

I heard one story about a child who smeared excrement all over the walls of her living room. Her mother tried to remove the mess and did not appear to be angry at all. But then, a few days later, the little girl spilled some orange juice on the table and her mother became extremely angry. Obviously the seeds of the anger had been sown or suppressed when the child smeared the excrement. So, if we are mindful we can deal with our anger before it becomes a bomb ready to explode.

If we were not able to transform our anger when it was just a seed, when the anger begins to arise, we can still transform it by following our breathing. If we cannot transform it immediately, it is best if we leave the situation and take refuge in walking meditation. The Plum Village community practices the Peace Treaty, an agreement between family or community members for what to do when we get angry.[2]

"Look at all beings with the eyes of compassion" is a quote from the *Lotus Sutra*. The eyes of compassion are also the eyes of understanding. Compassion is the sweet water that springs forth from the source of understanding. To practice looking deeply is the basic medicine for anger and hatred.

[2]　See Thich Nhat Hanh, *Touching Peace: Practicing the Art of Mindful Living* (Berkeley: Parallax Press, 1992).

THE SEVENTH MINDFULNESS TRAINING
DWELLING HAPPILY IN THE PRESENT MOMENT

Aware that life is available only in the present moment and that it is possible to live happily in the here and now, we are committed to training ourselves to live deeply each moment of daily life. We will try not to lose ourselves in dispersion or be carried away by regrets about the past, worries about the future, or craving, anger, or jealousy in the present. We will practice mindful breathing to come back to what is happening in the present moment. We are determined to learn the art of mindful living by touching the wondrous, refreshing, and healing elements that are inside and around us, and by nourishing seeds of joy, peace, love, and understanding in ourselves, thus facilitating the work of transformation and healing in our consciousness.

ॐ

We should try not to lose ourselves in dispersion or be carried away by regrets about the past, worries about the future, or craving, anger, or jealousy in the present. The Buddha offered us the practice of mindfulness to help us come back to what is happening in the present moment. Mindfulness allows us to touch the wondrous, refreshing, and healing elements that are inside and around us, and to nourish the seeds of joy, peace, love, and understanding in ourselves.

Like the kernel of a peach, this mindfulness training is at the heart of the life of the Order of Interbeing. Whether you live at a meditation center, work in an office, live with your family, or study at a university, the practice of mindfulness is crucial. The Chinese character for mindfulness has two components: heart, or mind, and present moment. To be mindful means to be fully present in the moment—not one part of you washing the dishes while another part is wondering when the work will be finished. Mindfulness can be practiced throughout the day. Walking, sitting, standing, lying down, working, and resting are all occasions for practice. Conscious breathing is the vehicle that brings us back to the present moment and keeps us here. The *Sutra on the Full Awareness of Breathing* and the *Sutra on the Four Establishments of Mindfulness* teach us how to be mindful in our body, our feelings, our mind, and the objects of our mind.

Mindfulness leads to concentration and wisdom. We develop concentration and wisdom along with a deep sense of joy and happiness because, as we see deeply into the nature of reality, we see how wonderful the world and the beings— animal, vegetal and mineral—that inhabit it are. Without mindfulness, we will not be in touch with the wonderful flowers, the glorious moon, our children, our spouse, or our friends. These are all infinitely precious and rare, part of the interbeing nature of all things. Mindfulness makes life real, deep, and worth living. It helps us be in the here and now where true life can be encountered. It helps us get in touch with refreshing and healing elements within and around us. While practicing this, we plant and water the seeds of joy, peace, and understanding in us, the seeds that have the power to modify and transform the pain and afflictions in us. It is not solely by touching these afflictions directly that we can heal them. Often these afflictions and pain can be transformed just because of the presence of the positive seeds that we plant and water in our daily life by the practice of mindful living.

In the *Pali Canon,* the term *dittha dhamma sukha vihari* is often used. It means to dwell happily in the present moment, in this very life. If we are not happy and joyful in our practice, it will become weak. Joy and happiness nourish our practice and make it stronger. If our practice does not transform our life and bring us great joy, if we are not able to bring joy to others and to understand them, we are not practicing correctly. The wonders of the universe are revealed to us in the meditation on interdependence. We can see that for one thing to exist, everything else also needs to exist. "This is, because that is."

The Fifth Mindfulness Training deals with greed, the Sixth with anger, and the Seventh deals with forgetfulness and the lack of understanding. The Fourteen Mindfulness Trainings of the Order of Interbeing follow and support one another like a string of pearls.

THE EIGHTH MINDFULNESS TRAINING
COMMUNITY AND COMMUNICATION

Aware that the lack of communication always brings separation and suffering, we are committed to training ourselves in the practice of compassionate listening and loving speech. We will learn to listen deeply without judging or reacting and refrain from uttering words that can create discord or cause the community to break. We will make every effort to keep communications open and to reconcile and resolve all conflicts, however small.

ॐ

The Eighth and Ninth Mindfulness Trainings deal with speech. The essence of the Eighth is concord. Community life is possible only with concord. The Buddha prescribed Six Concords, six principles of community life: living together in one place, sharing material resources, observing the same mindfulness trainings, practicing together and sharing the understanding of Dharma, reconciling differing viewpoints, and practicing kind speech to avoid all quarrels. These Six Concords have been practiced by Buddhist communities since the time of the Buddha and are still relevant. Even though the Eighth Mindfulness Training deals with speech, it relates directly to all of the Six Concords. When the first five concords are practiced, it is easy to observe loving speech. When there is good communication regarding ideas and interests, quarrels are not likely to occur.

Loving speech is born from understanding and patience. Practicing the Sixth Mindfulness Training, we found out that blaming does not help. Only understanding and love can bring about change. Reconciliation is an art, requiring us to understand both sides of a conflict. Not only do both sides bear partial responsibility, but even those of us who are not in the conflict bear some responsibility. If we had lived in mindfulness, we could have seen the earliest phases of the conflict beginning to arise, and we could have helped avoid it. To reconcile is not to judge by standing outside of a conflict. It is to take some responsibility for the existence of the conflict and to make every effort to understand the suffering of both sides. Then we can communicate to each side the suffering experienced by the other side, and offer some resolution based on an ideal common to both sides. The purpose of reconciliation is not to save face or for self-interest, but to realize understanding and compassion. To help reconcile, we ourselves must *embody* understanding and compassion.

Our awareness of the need for reconciliation and of our duty to work for it will empower us to act, and the success of our efforts will depend on the degree of our understanding and compassion, not only for the two sides, but for ourselves as well.

Every true community is a community of concord. Before a Buddhist community begins an activity like reciting the mindfulness trainings, making a decision, or performing the ceremony of mindfulness training transmission, the Sanghakarman Master always begins by asking, "Has the community gathered?"

"Yes, the community has gathered."

"Is there harmony in the community?"

"Yes, there is harmony in the community." If this is not the answer, the meeting cannot proceed. This practice is called *Sanghakarman Procedure,* established during the time of the Buddha, and has been practiced by communities of monks and nuns throughout the last twenty-five centuries.

THE NINTH MINDFULNESS TRAINING
TRUTHFUL AND LOVING SPEECH

Aware that words can create suffering or happiness, we are committed to learning to speak truthfully and construc- tively, using only words that inspire hope and confidence. We are determined not to say untruthful things for the sake of personal interest or to impress people, nor to utter words that might cause division or hatred. We will not spread news that we do not know to be certain nor criticize or condemn things of which we are not sure. We will do our best to speak out about situations of injustice, even when doing so may threaten our safety.

ॐ

This is the second mindfulness training dealing with speech. The words are simple and clear. When we speak, we can create a world of love, trust, and happiness, or a hell. We should be very careful about what we say and how we say it. If we are in the habit of talking too much, we should practice talking less. We must become aware of what we say and the results of our speaking. Even within Buddhist temples, we often speak too much, making comments about everything. All of us have experienced how negative speech can create a hell.

During retreats, we have the opportunity to practice silence, reducing our speaking by at least ninety percent. This practice can be extremely beneficial. Not only do we learn to control our speech, but we can reflect and see ourselves, the people around us, and life more clearly. When we have the opportunity to be in silence, we can look deeply and smile at the flowers, the grass, the bushes, the trees, the birds, and our fellow human beings. You who have observed periods of complete silence know the benefits of such practice. With silence, a smile, and right speech, we develop peace within ourselves and the world around us. Right speech is free of lying, gossip, exaggeration, harsh language, and foolish babble. Right speech builds understanding and reconciliation. The Ninth Mindfulness Training not only requires frankness from us, but courage as well. How many of us are brave enough to speak out about situations of injustice, even when doing so might threaten our own safety?

THE TENTH MINDFULNESS TRAINING
PROTECTING THE SANGHA

Aware that the essence and aim of a Sangha is the practice of understanding and compassion, we are determined not to use the Buddhist community for personal gain or profit or transform our community into a political instrument. A spiritual community should, however, take a clear stand against oppression and injustice and should strive to change the situation without engaging in partisan conflicts.

ॐ

Politicians often seek support from religious communities, but their aim is usually political. The purpose of a religious community is to guide people on the spiritual path. Therefore, to transform a religious community into a political party is to divert it from its true aim. Religious leaders may be tempted to support their government in exchange for the material well-being of their community. This has occurred throughout recorded history. In order to secure their government's support, religious communities often refrain from speaking out against oppression and injustices committed by their government. Allowing politicians to use your religious community to strengthen their political power is to surrender the spiritual sovereignty of your community.

"A spiritual community, however, should take a clear stand against oppression and injustice...." This should be done with a clear voice, based on the principles of the Four Noble Truths. The truth concerning the unjust situation should be fully exposed (the First Truth: suffering). The various causes of injustice should be enumerated (the Second Truth: the causes of suffering). The purpose and desire for removing the injustices should be made obvious (the Third Truth: the removal of suffering). The measures for removing the injustice should be proposed (the Fourth Truth: the way to end suffering). Although religious communities are not political powers, they can use their influence to change society. Speaking out is the first step, proposing and supporting appropriate measures for change is the next. Most important is to transcend all partisan conflicts. The voice of caring and understanding must be distinct from the voice of ambition.

THE ELEVENTH MINDFULNESS TRAINING
RIGHT LIVELIHOOD

Aware that great violence and injustice have been done to our environment and society, we are committed not to live with a vocation that is harmful to humans and nature. We will do our best to select a livelihood that helps realize our ideal of understanding and compassion. Aware of global economic, political and social realities, we will behave responsibly as consumers and as citizens, not investing in companies that deprive others of their chance to live.

ॐ

Right Livelihood is an element of the Noble Eightfold Path. It urges us to practice a profession that harms neither humans nor nature, physically or morally. Practicing mindfulness at work helps us discover whether our livelihood is right or not. We live in a society where jobs are hard to find and it is difficult to practice Right Livelihood. Still, if it happens that our work entails harming life, we should try our best to find another job. We should not drown in forgetfulness. Our vocation can nourish our understanding and compassion, or it can erode them. Our work has much to do with our practice of the Way.

Many modern industries, including food manufacturing, are harmful to humans and nature. Most current farming practices are far from Right Livelihood. The chemical poisons used by modern farmers harm the environment. Practicing Right Livelihood has become a difficult task for farmers. If they do not use chemical pesticides, it may be hard to compete commercially. Not many farmers have the courage to practice organic farming. Right Livelihood has ceased to be a purely personal matter. It is our collective karma.

Suppose I am a school teacher and I believe that nurturing love and understanding in children is a beautiful occupation, an example of Right Livelihood. I would object if someone asked me to stop teaching and become, for example, a butcher. However, if I meditate on the interrelatedness of all things, I will see that the butcher is not solely responsible for killing animals. He kills them for all of us who buy pieces of raw meat, cleanly wrapped and displayed at our local supermarket. The act of killing is a collective one. In forgetfulness, we may separate ourselves from the butcher, thinking his livelihood is wrong, while ours is right. However, if we didn't eat meat, the butcher wouldn't kill or would kill less. This is why Right Livelihood is a collective matter. The livelihood of each person affects all of us, and vice versa. The butcher's children may benefit from my teaching, while my children, because they eat meat, share some responsibility for the butcher's livelihood of killing.

Millions of people make a living off the arms industry, manufacturing "conventional" and nuclear weapons. These so-called conventional weapons are sold to Third World countries, most of them underdeveloped. People in these countries need food, not guns, tanks, or bombs. The United States, Russia, and the United Kingdom are the primary suppliers of these weapons. Manufacturing and selling weapons is certainly not Right Livelihood, but the responsibility for this situation does not lie solely with the workers in the arms industry. All of us—politicians, economists, and consumers—share the responsibility for the death and destruction caused by these weapons. We do not see clearly enough, we do not speak out, and we do not organize enough national debates on this huge problem. If we could discuss these issues globally, solutions could be found. New jobs must be created so that we do not have to live on the profits of weapons manufacturing.

If we are able to work in a profession that helps us realize our ideal of compassion, we should be very grateful. Every day, we should help create proper jobs for ourselves and others by living correctly—simply and sanely. To awaken ourselves and others and to help ourselves and others are the essence of Mahayana Buddhism. Individual karma cannot be separated from collective karma. If you have the opportunity, please use your energy to improve both. This is the realization of the first of the Four Great Vows.

THE TWELFTH MINDFULNESS TRAINING
REVERENCE FOR LIFE

Aware that much suffering is caused by war and conflict, we are determined to cultivate nonviolence, understanding, and compassion in our daily lives, to promote peace education, mindful mediation, and reconciliation within families, communities, nations, and in the world. We are determined not to kill and not to let others kill. We will diligently practice deep looking with our Sangha to discover better ways to protect life and prevent war.

༄

In every country in the world, killing human beings is condemned. The Buddhist training to practice non-killing extends even further, to include all living beings. However, no one, not even a Buddha or a bodhisattva, can practice this mindfulness training to perfection. When we take a small step or boil a cup of water, we kill many tiny living beings. The essence of this training is to make every effort to respect and protect life, to continuously move in the direction of peace and reconciliation. We can try our best, even if we cannot succeed one hundred percent.

This mindfulness training is closely linked with the Eleventh. Our patterns of livelihood and consuming have very much to do with the lives and security of humans and other living beings. There are many types of violence. Among societies, it manifests as war—often caused by fanaticism and narrowness or by the will to gain political influence or economic power. Or violence can be the exploitation of one society by another that is technologically or politically stronger. We can oppose wars once they have started, but it is better to also do our best to prevent wars from breaking out. The way to prevent war is to make peace. We accomplish this first in our daily life by combating fanaticism and attachment to views, and working for social justice. We have to work vigorously against the political and economic ambitions of any country, including our own. If important issues like these are not debated on national and international levels, we will never be able to prevent societal violence.

We begin by studying and practicing this mindfulness training of non-killing in our daily lives, and then we can work to bring out the real issues of violence and peace to the whole nation. If we do not live our daily lives mindfully, we ourselves are responsible, to some extent, for the structural violence. The amount of grain used in Western countries to make liquor and feed cattle, for example, is enormous. Professor François Peroux, director of the Institute of Applied Mathematics and Economics in Paris, has suggested that by reducing meat and alcohol consumption in the West by fifty percent, the grains that would become available would be enough to solve all hunger and malnutrition problems in the Third World. Deaths caused by automobile accidents and cardiovascular illnesses would also be reduced in the West if the consumption of liquor and meat would decrease.

Defense budgets in Western countries continue to be mammoth, even after the post-Cold War spending cuts. Studies show that if we could stop or significantly slow down the manufacture of weapons, we would have more than enough money to erase poverty, hunger, many diseases, and ignorance from the world. In our busy daily lives, do we have enough time to look deeply into this mindfulness training of non-killing? How many among us can honestly say that we are doing enough to practice this training?

THE THIRTEENTH MINDFULNESS TRAINING
GENEROSITY

Aware of the suffering caused by exploitation, social injustice, stealing, and oppression, we are committed to cultivating loving kindness and learning ways to work for the well-being of people, animals, plants, and minerals. We will practice generosity by sharing our time, energy, and material resources with those who are in need. We are determined not to steal and not to possess anything that should belong to others. We will respect the property of others, but will try to prevent others from profiting from human suffering or the suffering of other beings.

ୡ

Bringing to our awareness the pain caused by social injustice, the Thirteenth Mindfulness Training urges us to work for a more livable society. This training is closely linked with to Fourth (Awareness of Suffering), the Fifth (Simple, Healthy Living), the Eleventh (Right Livelihood), and the Twelfth (Reverence for Life). In order to understand this mindfulness training deeply, we need to meditate on those four other trainings.

Exploitation, social injustice, stealing, and oppression come in many forms and cause much suffering. The moment we commit ourselves to cultivating loving kindness, loving kindness is born in us, and we make every effort to stop these things. Loving kindness (*maitri* in Sanskrit, *metta* in Pali) is the intention and capacity to bring joy and happi-

ness to another person or living being. But even with maitri
as a source of energy in us, we still need to learn to find ways
to express it. We have to work as individuals and come together as a community to examine our situation, exercising
our intelligence and ability to look deeply so that we can discover appropriate ways to express maitri in the midst of real
problems.

Suppose we want to help those who are suffering under a
dictatorship. We know that sending in troops to overthrow
their government will cause the deaths of many innocent
people. By looking more deeply, with loving kindness, we
may realize that the best time to help is before a country falls
into the hands of a dictator. Offering young people of that
country the opportunity to learn democratic ways of gov-
erning would be a good investment for peace in the future.
If we wait until the situation gets bad, it may be too late. If
we practice together with politicians, soldiers, businessmen,
lawyers, legislators, artists, writers, and teachers, we can find
the best ways to practice compassion, loving kindness, and
understanding.

The feeling of generosity and the capacity for being gen-
erous are not enough. We need to practice our generosity.
This takes time. We may want to help others be happy, but
we are caught in the problems of our own daily lives. Sometimes one pill or a little rice could save the life of a sick or
hungry child, but we may think we do not have the time to
help. It costs only about twenty cents to provide both lunch
and dinner for a poor child in many countries. There are
many simple things like this we can do to help people, but
we do nothing because we think we cannot free ourselves
from our busy lifestyles.

Developing ways to prevent others from profiting from human suffering is the primary duty of legislators, politicians, and revolutionary leaders. However, each of us can also act in this direction. To some degree, we can stay close to oppressed people and help them protect their right to life and defend themselves against oppression and exploitation. The bodhisattva vows are immense, and each of us can vow to sit with the bodhisattvas on their life rafts.

THE FOURTEENTH MINDFULNESS TRAINING
RIGHT CONDUCT

(For lay members): Aware that sexual relations motivated by craving cannot dissipate the feeling of loneliness but will create more suffering, frustration, and isolation, we are determined not to engage in sexual relations without mutual understanding, love, and a long-term commitment. In sexual relations, we must be aware of future suffering that may be caused. We know that to preserve the happiness of ourselves and others, we must respect the rights and commitments of ourselves and others. We will do everything in our power to protect children from sexual abuse and to protect couples and families from being broken by sexual misconduct. We will treat our bodies with respect and preserve our vital energies (sexual, breath, spirit) for the realization of our bodhisattva ideal. We will be fully aware of the responsibility of bringing new lives into the world, and will meditate on the world into which we are bringing new beings.

(For monastic members): Aware that the aspiration of a monk or a nun can only be realized when he or she wholly leaves behind the bonds of worldly love, we are committed to practic-

ing chastity and to helping others protect themselves. We are aware that loneliness and suffering cannot be alleviated by the coming together of two bodies in a sexual relationship, but by the practice of true understanding and compassion. We know that a sexual relationship will destroy our life as a monk or a nun, will prevent us from realizing our ideal of serving living beings, and will harm others. We are determined not to suppress or mistreat our body or to look upon our body as only an instrument, but to learn to handle our body with respect. We are determined to preserve vital energies (sexual, breath, spirit) for the realization of our bodhisattva ideal.

ॐ

So many individuals, children, couples, and families have been wounded by sexual misconduct. Practicing this training is to prevent ourselves and others from being wounded. Our stability and the stability of our families and society depend on it. To practice the Fourteenth Mindfulness Training is to heal ourselves and our society. When we are determined in this effort, the energy that is born helps us transform into a bodhisattva. This is mindful living.

In Buddhism, we speak of the oneness of body and spirit. Whatever happens to the body also happens to the spirit. The sanity of the body is the sanity of the spirit; the violation of the body is the violation of the spirit. The union of the two bodies can only be positive when there is also understanding and communion on the level of the spirit.

Sexual communion should be a ritual performed in mindfulness with great respect, care, and love. True love contains care and respect. It is deep, beautiful, and whole. In my tradition, husband and wife are expected to respect each other like guests, and when they practice this kind of respect, their love and happiness will continue for a long time. In sexual relationships, respect is one of the most important elements.

True love also includes the sense of responsibility, accepting the other person as they are, with all their strengths and weaknesses. The expression "long-term commitment" helps us understand the word "love." A long-term commitment between two people is only the beginning. For a tree to be strong, it needs to send many roots deep into the soil. If a tree has only one root, it may be blown over by the wind. The life of a couple also needs to be supported by many elements—families, friends, ideals, practice, and Sangha. Understanding this training in the context of community is very important.

"Responsibility" is the key word. We need mindfulness in order to have that sense of responsibility. In a community of practice, if there is no sexual misconduct, if the community practices this mindfulness training well, there will be stability and peace. You respect, support, and protect each other as Dharma brothers and sisters. Otherwise, you may become irresponsible and create trouble. We refrain from sexual misconduct because we are responsible for the well-being of so many people. If we are irresponsible, we can destroy everything. Practicing this training, we keep the Sangha beautiful.

We need to discuss problems relating to the practice of this training, like loneliness, advertising, and even the sex industry. The feeling of loneliness is universal in our society. When there is no communication between ourselves and other people, even in the family, the feeling of loneliness may push us into having sexual relationships. The belief that having a sexual relationship will help us feel less lonely is a kind of superstition. In fact, we will be more lonely afterwards. When there is not enough communication with another person on the level of the heart and spirit, a sexual relationship will only widen the gap and destroy us both. Our relationship will be stormy, and we will make each other suffer.

In practicing the Fourteenth Mindfulness Training, we should always look into the nature of our love in order to see and not be fooled by our feelings. Sometimes we feel that we have love for the other person, but maybe that love is only an attempt to satisfy our egoistic needs. Maybe we have not looked deeply enough to see the needs of the other person. He or she should not be looked upon as an object of our desire or some kind of commercial item. Sex is used pervasively in our society as a means for selling products. There is also the sex industry. These things are obstacles to our practice. We must remember to look at one another as human beings with the capacity of becoming a Buddha.

After several years of ascetic practice, Shakyamuni Buddha realized that mistreating his body was a mistake, and he abandoned that practice. He saw that both indulging in sensual pleasure and mistreating his body were extremes to be avoided, that both lead to degeneration of mind and body. As a result, he adopted a Middle Way between the two extremes.

In Asia, we say there are three sources of energy—sexual, breath, and spirit. Sexual energy is the type of energy that we expend during sexual intercourse. Vital breath is the energy we expend when we speak too much and breathe too little. Spirit is the energy we expend when we worry too much.

We need to know how to maintain the balance, or we may act irresponsibly. According to Oriental medicine, if these three sources of energy are depleted, the body will weaken and disease will appear. Then it will be more difficult to practice. In Taoism and also in the martial arts, there are practices for preserving and nourishing these three sources of energy.

When practicing conscious breathing—counting the breath or following the breath—we do not waste the vital breath energy, instead we strengthen it. Concentration and the enjoyment of meditation do not expend spirit, but strengthen it. You can learn ways to channel your sexual energy into deep realizations in the domains of art and meditation.

In the Buddha's time, a typical monk was a quiet person who practiced walking and sitting meditation both day and night. He carried a bowl into the local villages every morning to beg for food and would give a short Dharma talk to each layperson who donated some food. This way of life enabled him to preserve both vital breath and spirit. In the time of the Buddha, the main reason for monks abstaining from sexual activity was to preserve energy. This is a point of commonality between Buddhism and most other Eastern spiritual and medical traditions. During the most difficult periods of his nonviolent struggles, Mahatma Gandhi also practiced abstinence, and he advised his colleagues to do the same in coping with tense, difficult situations. Strength of spirit depends on these three sources of energy. In Vietnamese, the word "spiritual" *(tinh thân)* is formed by combining the words for sexual energy *(tinh)* and spirit *(thân)*. The material and the spiritual are no longer distinct, and the name of each is used for the other. Those who have fasted know that if the three sources of energy are not preserved, you cannot fast for long. In 1966, the monk Thich Tri Quang fasted in Vietnam for one hundred days, because he knew how to preserve his three sources of energy.

A second reason that monks in the Buddha's time refrained from sexual activity was that they wanted to concentrate on their career of enlightenment. If a monk had a family to support and take care of, he would have had little time left for practice. Today many monks and priests are continually busy, whether or not they have wives or children. Just having to take care of their temples and religious communities, they are as busy as householders. One day the monk Dai San complained to his friend that he was too busy, and his friend replied, "Why don't you become a monk?" A monk is not supposed to be so busy. If he has no time to practice, there is really no reason to remain a monk.

A third reason that monks in the Buddha's time refrained from sexuality was to cut off "the chain of rebirth" *(samsara)*. The first meaning of rebirth means to be reborn in our offspring, our children and grandchildren. During the time of the Buddha, much more so than in our own time, poverty and disease were the common lot for most people. This situation is reflected in the First Noble Truth. Imagine a family with too many children, all of them frail and ill. There is a permanent shortage of food, no medicine, and no means of contraception. Each year a new child is born. This is still common in many parts of our world, and both parents and children suffer. Rebirth must be understood in this context and with this background. For these people, a new birth is often not a joy, but a catastrophe. To give birth to a child is to perpetuate the cycle of hunger and disease. This is the continuation of samsara. The mindfulness training for celibacy during the time of the Buddha also aimed at preventing childbirth; it had a birth-control function.

Therefore, this mindfulness training is directly related to issues of population, hunger, and economic development. The presence of Buddhist monks in countries like Sri Lanka, Burma, Thailand, Laos, Cambodia, China, Vietnam, Korea, Tibet, Mongolia, and Japan for more than twenty centuries has contributed significantly to reducing the world's population by billions. The population explosion is one of the most serious problems of our day. Hunger leads to war and, in our times, wars are incredibly destructive. Countries that cannot control their populations cannot overcome poverty. And there is the threat of nuclear holocaust. Parents must be aware of the actual situation of the world. We should know the future into which we are sending our children, to motivate us to act and live in a way that can create a better future for ourselves and our children.

We must be clearly aware of the responsibility we bear in bringing new life into the world. The answer is not to stop having children, but to make the world a better place. The future of the Earth and our children depends on the way we live today. If we continue to exploit and destroy our ecosystems, if we allow the arms race to continue, if we do not curb the growth of the world's population, the Earth and humankind will not have a future. Each of our ways of life can be a brick for building a future of peace. The Fourteenth Mindfulness Training is vast, and its observance is linked to all the other mindfulness trainings of the Order of Interbeing. To understand and practice this training deeply, we have to see the relationship between it and our daily meditation practice, the Four Noble Truths, and the Buddhist teaching on rebirth.

ஒ

The Fourteen Mindfulness Trainings of the Order of Interbeing are the heart of the Buddha. They are mindfulness in our real lives and not just the teaching of ideas. If we practice these trainings deeply, we will recognize that each of them contains all the others. Studying and practicing the mindfulness trainings can help us understand the true nature of interbeing—we cannot just be by ourselves alone; we can only inter-be with everyone and everything else. To practice these trainings is to become aware of what is going on in our bodies, our minds, and the world. With awareness, we can live our lives happily, fully present in each moment we are alive, intelligently seeking solutions to the problems we face, and working for peace in small and large ways.

When you practice the Five Mindfulness Trainings[3] deeply, you are already practicing the Fourteen. If you want to formally receive the Fourteen Mindfulness Trainings and enter the core community of the Order of Interbeing, it is because you wish to become a community leader, to organize the practice in a Sangha. Only when you have the feeling that you have enough time, energy, and interest to take care of a community should you ask for formal ordination. Then you will be working together with other brothers

---

[3] Five Mindfulness Trainings, see pp. 67-71.

and sisters. Otherwise, the Five Mindfulness Trainings are enough. You can practice the Fourteen without a formal ceremony, without being ordained as a member of the Order.

Many people of all religious faiths love the Fourteen Mindfulness Trainings. You can modify a few words if you like, so it applies to Christian, Jewish, Islamic, or other teachings. I hope you will join me in practicing these mindfulness trainings or the equivalent from your own tradition. It is crucial for our own well-being and the well-being of our world.

PART THREE

Ceremonies

Ceremonies

1

INCENSE OFFERING

Head of Ceremony: In gratitude, we offer this incense to all Buddhas and bodhisattvas throughout space and time. May it be fragrant as Earth herself, reflecting our careful efforts, our wholehearted awareness, and the fruit of understanding, slowly ripening in us. May we and all beings be companions of Buddhas and bodhisattvas. May we awaken from forgetfulness and realize our true home.

(bell)

TOUCHING THE EARTH

Teaching and living the way of awareness in the very midst of suffering and confusion, Shakyamuni Buddha, the Enlightened One, to whom we bow in gratitude.

(bell)

Cutting through ignorance, awakening our hearts and minds, Manjushri, the Bodhisattva of Great Understanding, to whom we bow in gratitude.

(bell)

Working mindfully and joyfully for the sake of all beings, Samantabhadra, the Bodhisattva of Great Action, to whom we bow in gratitude.

(bell)

Responding to suffering, serving beings in countless ways, Avalokiteshvara, the Bodhisattva of Great Compassion, to whom we bow in gratitude.

(bell)

Seed of awakening and loving kindness in children and all beings, Maitreya, the Buddha To Be Born, to whom we bow in gratitude.

(bell)

Showing the way fearlessly and compassionately, the stream of ancestral teachers, to whom we bow in gratitude.

(two sounds of the bell)

OPENING CHANT

(Head of Ceremony chants each line, echoed by whole assembly):

The Dharma is deep and lovely.
We now have a chance to see it,
study it, and practice it.
We vow to realize its true meaning.

INTRODUCTORY WORDS

Today the community has gathered to recite the Three Jewels, the Two Promises, the Five Mindfulness Trainings, and the Fourteen Mindfulness Trainings of the Order of Interbeing. First we will recite the Three Jewels and the Two Promises. Will the younger members of the community please come forward.

Young people, upon hearing the sound of the bell, please bow three times to show your gratitude to the Buddha, the Dharma, and the Sangha.

(bell)

THE THREE JEWELS

Young students of the Buddha, you have taken refuge in the Buddha, the one who shows you the way in this life; in the Dharma, the way of understanding and love; and in the Sangha, the community that lives in harmony and awareness. It is beneficial to recite the Three Jewels regularly. Will the entire community please join with the young people in repeating after me:

> *I take refuge in the Buddha,*
> *the one who shows me the way in this life.*
> *I take refuge in the Dharma,*
> *the way of understanding and love.*
> *I take refuge in the Sangha,*
> *the community that lives in harmony and*
> *awareness.*

THE TWO PROMISES

Young students of the Buddha, we have completed the recitation of the Three Jewels. Now we will recite the Two Promises that you have made with the Buddha, the Dharma, and the Sangha. Will the entire community please join the young people in repeating after me:

> *I vow to develop understanding,*
> *in order to live peaceably*
> *with people, animals, plants, and minerals.*

This is the first promise you have made with the Buddha, our teacher. Have you tried to learn more about it and to keep your promise during the past two weeks?

(bell)

I vow to develop my compassion,
in order to protect the lives
of people, animals, plants, and minerals.

This is the second promise you have made with the Buddha, our teacher. Have you tried to learn more about it and to keep your promise during the past two weeks?

(bell)

Young students of the Enlightened One, understanding and love are the two most important teachings of the Buddha. If we do not make the effort to be open, to understand the suffering of other people, we will not be able to love them and to live in harmony with them. We should also try to understand and protect the lives of animals, plants, and minerals and live in harmony with them. If we cannot understand, we cannot love. The Buddha teaches us to look at living beings with the eyes of love and understanding. Please learn to practice this teaching.

Young people, upon hearing the sound of the bell, please bow three times to the Three Jewels, and then you can leave the Meditation Hall.

(three sounds of the bell)

2

RECITING THE FIVE MINDFULNESS TRAININGS

(This ceremony should begin with Incense Offering, Touching the Earth, and Opening Chant from pages 63–64.)

SANGHAKARMAN PROCEDURE

Sanghakarman Master: Has the entire community assembled?

Sanghakarman Convener: The entire community has assembled.

Sanghakarman Master: Is there harmony in the community?

Sanghakarman Convener: Yes, there is harmony.

Sanghakarman Master: Is there anyone not able to be present who has asked to be represented, and have they declared themselves to have done their best to study and practice the Five Mindfulness Trainings?

Sanghakarman Convener: No, there is not.

or

Sanghakarman Convener: Yes, _____(name)_____, for health reasons, cannot be at the recitation today. She has asked _____(name)_____ to represent her and she declares that she has done her best to study and practice the mindfulness trainings.

Sanghakarman Master: What is the reason for the community gathering today?

Sanghakarman Convener: The community has gathered to practice the recitation of the Five Mindfulness Trainings. Noble community, please listen. Today, _____(date)_____, has been declared to be the Mindfulness Training Recitation Day. We have gathered at the appointed time. The noble community is ready to hear and recite the mindfulness trainings in an atmosphere of harmony, and the recitation can proceed.

Is that correct?

Everyone: That is correct.

(repeat question and answer three times)

INTRODUCTORY WORDS

Brothers and Sisters, it is now time to recite the Five Mindfulness Trainings. Please, those who have been ordained as *Upasaka* and *Upasika* kneel with joined palms in the direction of the Buddha, our teacher.

Brothers and Sisters, please listen. The Five Mindfulness Trainings are the basis for a happy life. They have the capacity to protect life and to make it beautiful and worth living. They are also the door that opens to enlightenment and liberation. Please listen to each mindfulness training, and answer yes, silently every time you see that you have made the effort to study, practice, and observe it.

THE FIVE MINDFULNESS TRAININGS

THE FIRST OF THE FIVE MINDFULNESS TRAININGS

Aware of the suffering caused by the destruction of life, I am committed to cultivating compassion and learning ways to protect the lives of people, animals, plants, and minerals. I am determined not to kill, not to let others kill, and not to condone any act of killing in the world, in my thinking, and in my way of life.

(silence)

This is the first of the Five Mindfulness Trainings. Have you made an effort to study and practice it during the past two weeks?

(bell)

THE SECOND OF THE FIVE MINDFULNESS TRAININGS

Aware of the suffering caused by exploitation, social injustice, stealing, and oppression, I am committed to cultivating loving kindness and learning ways to work for the well-being of people, animals, plants, and minerals. I will practice generosity by sharing my time, energy, and material resources with those who are in real need. I am determined not to steal and not to possess anything that should belong to others. I will respect the property of others, but I will prevent others from profiting from human suffering or the suffering of other species on Earth.

(silence)

This is the second of the Five Mindfulness Trainings. Have you made an effort to study and practice it during the past two weeks?

(bell)

THE THIRD OF THE FIVE MINDFULNESS TRAININGS

Aware of the suffering caused by sexual misconduct, I am committed to cultivating responsibility and learning ways to protect the safety and integrity of individuals, couples, families, and society. I am determined not to engage in sexual relations without love and a long-term commitment. To preserve the happiness of myself and others, I am determined to respect my commitments and the commitments of others. I will do everything in my power to protect children from sexual abuse and to prevent couples and families from being broken by sexual misconduct.

(silence)

This is the third of the Five Mindfulness Trainings. Have you made an effort to study and practice it during the past two weeks?

(bell)

THE FOURTH OF THE FIVE MINDFULNESS TRAININGS

Aware of the suffering caused by unmindful speech and the inability to listen to others, I am committed to cultivating loving speech and deep listening in order to bring joy and happiness to others and relieve others of their suffering. Knowing that words can create happiness or suffering, I am determined to speak truthfully, with words that inspire self-confidence, joy, and hope. I will not spread news that I do not know to be certain and will not criticize or condemn things of which I am not sure. I will refrain from uttering words that can cause division or discord, or that can cause the family or the community to break. I am determined to make all efforts to reconcile and resolve all conflicts, however small.

(silence)

This is the fourth of the Five Mindfulness Trainings. Have you made an effort to study and practice it during the past two weeks?

(bell)

THE FIFTH OF THE FIVE MINDFULNESS TRAININGS

Aware of the suffering caused by unmindful consumption, I am committed to cultivating good health, both physical and mental, for myself, my family, and my society by practicing mindful eating, drinking, and consuming. I will ingest only items that preserve peace, well-being, and joy in my body, in my consciousness, and in the collective body and consciousness of my family and society. I am determined not to use alcohol or any other intoxicant or to ingest foods or other items that contain toxins, such as certain TV programs, magazines, books, films, and conversations. I am aware that to damage my body or my consciousness with these poisons is to betray my ancestors, my parents, my society, and future generations. I will work to transform violence, fear, anger, and confusion in myself and in society by practicing a diet for myself and for society. I understand that a proper diet is crucial for self-transformation and for the transformation of society.

(silence)

This is the fifth of the Five Mindfulness Trainings. Have you made an effort to study and practice it during the past two weeks?

(bell)

CONCLUDING WORDS

Brothers and Sisters, we have recited the Five Mindfulness Trainings, the foundation of happiness for the individual, the family, and society. We should recite them regularly so that our study and practice of the mindfulness trainings can deepen day by day.

Please join your palms and recite each line of the closing chant after me:

> *Reciting the trainings,*
> *practicing the way of awareness,*
> *gives rise to benefits without limit.*
> *We vow to share the fruits with all beings.*
> *We vow to offer tribute to parents, teachers,*
> *friends, and numerous beings*
> *who give guidance and support along the path.*

3
RECITING THE FOURTEEN MINDFULNESS TRAININGS
OF THE ORDER OF INTERBEING

INCENSE OFFERING

Head of Ceremony: In gratitude, we offer this incense to all Buddhas and bodhisattvas throughout space and time. May it be fragrant as Earth herself, reflecting our careful efforts, our wholehearted awareness, and the fruit of understanding, slowly ripening in us. May we and all beings be companions of Buddhas and bodhisattvas. May we awaken from forgetfulness and realize our true home.

(bell)

TOUCHING THE EARTH

Teaching and living the way of awareness in the very midst of suffering and confusion, Shakyamuni Buddha, the Enlightened One, to whom we bow in gratitude.

(bell)

Cutting through ignorance, awakening our hearts and minds, Manjushri, the Bodhisattva of Great Understanding, to whom we bow in gratitude.

(bell)

Working mindfully and joyfully for the sake of all beings, Samantabhadra, the Bodhisattva of Great Action, to whom we bow in gratitude.

(bell)

Responding to suffering, serving beings in countless ways, Avalokiteshvara, the Bodhisattva of Great Compassion, to whom we bow in gratitude.

(bell)

Seed of awakening and loving kindness in children and all beings, Maitreya, the Buddha To Be Born, to whom we bow in gratitude.

(bell)

Showing the way fearlessly and compassionately, the stream of ancestral teachers, to whom we bow in gratitude.

(two sounds of the bell)

OPENING CHANT

(Head of Ceremony chants each line, echoed by whole assembly):

> *The Dharma is deep and lovely.*
> *We now have a chance to see it,*
> *study it, and practice it.*
> *We vow to realize its true meaning.*

SANGHAKARMAN PROCEDURE

Sanghakarman Master: Has the whole community assembled?

Sanghakarman Convener: The whole community has assembled.

Sanghakarman Master: Is there harmony in the community?

Sanghakarman Convener: Yes, there is harmony.

Sanghakarman Master: Is there anyone not able to be present who has asked to be represented, and have they declared themselves to have done their best to study and practice the mindfulness trainings?

Sanghakarman Convener: No, there is not.

or

Sanghakarman Convener: Yes, Brother (or Sister) __(name)__, for health reasons, cannot be at the recitation today. He has asked Brother (or Sister) __(name)__ to represent him and he declares that he has done his best to study and practice the mindfulness trainings.

Sanghakarman Master: Why has the community assembled today?

Sanghakarman Convener: The community has assembled to practice the recitation of the Fourteen Mindfulness Trainings of the Order of Interbeing. Noble community, please listen. Today, __(date)__, has been declared as the day to recite the Fourteen Mindfulness Trainings of the Order of Interbeing. The community has assembled at the appointed time and is ready to hear and to recite the Fourteen Mindfulness Trainings in an atmosphere of harmony. Thus, the recitation can proceed.

Is that correct?

Everyone: That is correct.

(repeat question and answer three times)

INTRODUCTORY WORDS

Today I have been asked by the community to recite the mindfulness trainings. I ask the community for spiritual support. Please, Brothers and Sisters, listen.

The mindfulness trainings are the very essence of the Order of Interbeing. They are the torch lighting our path, the boat carrying us, the teacher guiding us. I ask the community to listen with a serene mind. Consider the mindfulness trainings as a clear mirror in which to look at ourselves. Say yes, silently, every time you see that during the past week you have made an effort to learn, practice, and observe the mindfulness training read.

(bell)

Brothers and Sisters, are you ready?

Everyone (silently): I am ready.

THE FOURTEEN MINDFULNESS TRAININGS

These then are the Fourteen Mindfulness Trainings of the Order of Interbeing.

THE FIRST MINDFULNESS TRAINING

Aware of the suffering created by fanaticism and intolerance, we are determined not to be idolatrous about or bound to any doctrine, theory, or ideology, even Buddhist ones. Buddhist teachings are guiding means to help us learn to look deeply and to develop our understanding and compassion. They are not doctrines to fight, kill, or die for.

(silence)

This is the First Mindfulness Training of the Order of Interbeing. Have you studied, practiced, and observed it during the past two weeks?

(bell)

THE SECOND MINDFULNESS TRAINING

Aware of the suffering created by attachment to views and wrong perceptions, we are determined to avoid being narrow-minded and bound to present views. We shall learn and practice nonattachment from views in order to be open to others' insights and experiences. We are aware that the knowledge we presently possess is not changeless, absolute truth. Truth is found in life, and we will observe life within and around us in every moment, ready to learn throughout our lives.

(silence)

This is the Second Mindfulness Training of the Order of Interbeing. Have you studied, practiced, and observed it during the past two weeks?

(bell)

THE THIRD MINDFULNESS TRAINING

Aware of the suffering brought about when we impose our views on others, we are committed not to force others, even our children, by any means whatsoever—such as authority, threat, money, propaganda, or indoctrination—to adopt our views. We will respect the right of others to be different and to choose what to believe and how to decide. We will, however, help others renounce fanaticism and narrowness through compassionate dialogue.

(silence)

This is the Third Mindfulness Training of the Order of Interbeing. Have you studied, practiced, and observed it during the past two weeks?

(bell)

THE FOURTH MINDFULNESS TRAINING

Aware that looking deeply at the nature of suffering can help us develop compassion and find ways out of suffering, we are determined not to avoid or close our eyes before suffering. We are committed to finding ways, including personal contact, images, and sounds, to be with those who suffer, so we can understand their situation deeply and help them transform their suffering into compassion, peace, and joy.

(silence)

This is the Fourth Mindfulness Training of the Order of Interbeing. Have you studied, practiced, and observed it during the past two weeks?

(bell)

THE FIFTH MINDFULNESS TRAINING

Aware that true happiness is rooted in peace, solidity, freedom, and compassion, and not in wealth or fame, we are determined not to take as the aim of our life fame, profit, wealth, or sensual pleasure, nor to accumulate wealth while millions are hungry and dying. We are committed to living simply and sharing our time, energy, and material resources with those in need. We will practice mindful consuming, not using alcohol, drugs, or any other products that bring toxins into our own and the collective body and consciousness.

(silence)

This is the Fifth Mindfulness Training of the Order of Interbeing. Have you studied, practiced, and observed it during the past two weeks?

(bell)

THE SIXTH MINDFULNESS TRAINING

Aware that anger blocks communication and creates suffering, we are determined to take care of the energy of anger when it arises and to recognize and transform the seeds of anger that lie deep in our consciousness. When anger comes up, we are determined not to do or say anything, but to practice mindful breathing or mindful walking and acknowledge, embrace, and look deeply into our anger. We will learn to look with the eyes of compassion at those we think are the cause of our anger.

(silence)

This is the Sixth Mindfulness Training of the Order of Interbeing. Have you studied, practiced, and observed it during the past two weeks?

(bell)

THE SEVENTH MINDFULNESS TRAINING

Aware that life is available only in the present moment and that it is possible to live happily in the here and now, we are committed to training ourselves to live deeply each moment of daily life. We will try not to lose ourselves in dispersion or be carried away by regrets about the past, worries about the future, or craving, anger, or jealousy in the present. We will practice mindful breathing to come back to what is happening in the present moment. We are determined to learn the art of mindful living by touching the wondrous, refreshing, and healing elements that are inside and around us, and by nourishing seeds of joy, peace, love, and understanding in ourselves, thus facilitating the work of transformation and healing in our consciousness.

(silence)

This is the Seventh Mindfulness Training of the Order of Interbeing. Have you studied, practiced, and observed it during the past two weeks?

(bell)

THE EIGHTH MINDFULNESS TRAINING

Aware that the lack of communication always brings separation and suffering, we are committed to training ourselves in the practice of compassionate listening and loving speech. We will learn to listen deeply without judging or reacting and refrain from uttering words that can create discord or cause the community to break. We will make every effort to keep communications open and to reconcile and resolve all conflicts, however small.

(silence)

This is the Eighth Mindfulness Training of the Order of Interbeing. Have you studied, practiced, and observed it during the past two weeks?

(bell)

THE NINTH MINDFULNESS TRAINING

Aware that words can create suffering or happiness, we are committed to learning to speak truthfully and constructively, using only words that inspire hope and confidence. We are determined not to say untruthful things for the sake of personal interest or to impress people, nor to utter words that might cause division or hatred. We will not spread news that we do not know to be certain nor criticize or condemn things of which we are not sure. We will do our best to speak out about situations of injustice, even when doing so may threaten our safety.

(silence)

This is the Ninth Mindfulness Training of the Order of Interbeing. Have you studied, practiced, and observed it during the past two weeks?

(bell)

THE TENTH MINDFULNESS TRAINING

Aware that the essence and aim of a Sangha is the practice of understanding and compassion, we are determined not to use the Buddhist community for personal gain or profit or transform our community into a political instrument. A spiritual community should, however, take a clear stand against oppression and injustice and should strive to change the situation without engaging in partisan conflicts.

(silence)

This is the Tenth Mindfulness Training of the Order of Interbeing. Have you studied, practiced, and observed it during the past two weeks?

(bell)

THE ELEVENTH MINDFULNESS TRAINING

Aware that great violence and injustice have been done to our environment and society, we are committed not to live with a vocation that is harmful to humans and nature. We will do our best to select a livelihood that helps realize our ideal of understanding and compassion. Aware of global economic, political and social realities, we will behave responsibly as consumers and as citizens, not investing in companies that deprive others of their chance to live.

(silence)

This is the Eleventh Mindfulness Training of the Order of Interbeing. Have you studied, practiced, and observed it during the past two weeks?

(bell)

THE TWELFTH MINDFULNESS TRAINING

Aware that much suffering is caused by war and conflict, we are determined to cultivate nonviolence, understanding, and compassion in our daily lives, to promote peace education, mindful mediation, and reconciliation within families, communities, nations, and in the world. We are determined not to kill and not to let others kill. We will diligently practice deep looking with our Sangha to discover better ways to protect life and prevent war.

(silence)

This is the Twelfth Mindfulness Training of the Order of Interbeing. Have you studied, practiced, and observed it during the past two weeks?

(bell)

THE THIRTEENTH MINDFULNESS TRAINING

Aware of the suffering caused by exploitation, social injustice, stealing, and oppression, we are committed to cultivating loving kindness and learning ways to work for the well-being of people, animals, plants, and minerals. We will practice generosity by sharing our time, energy, and material resources with those who are in need. We are determined not to steal and not to possess anything that should belong to others. We will respect the property of others, but will try to prevent others from profiting from human suffering or the suffering of other beings.

(silence)

This is the Thirteenth Mindfulness Training of the Order of Interbeing. Have you studied, practiced, and observed it during the past two weeks?

(bell)

THE FOURTEENTH MINDFULNESS TRAINING

(For lay members): Aware that sexual relations motivated by craving cannot dissipate the feeling of loneliness but will create more suffering, frustration, and isolation, we are determined not to engage in sexual relations without mutual understanding, love, and a long-term commitment. In sexual relations, we must be aware of future suffering that may be caused. We know that to preserve the happiness of ourselves and others, we must respect the rights and commitments of ourselves and others. We will do everything in our power to protect children from sexual abuse and to protect couples and families from being broken by sexual misconduct. We will treat our bodies with respect and preserve our vital energies (sexual, breath, spirit) for the realization of our bodhisattva ideal. We will be fully aware of the responsibility of bringing new lives into the world, and will meditate on the world into which we are bringing new beings.

(For monastic members): Aware that the aspiration of a monk or a nun can only be realized when he or she wholly leaves behind the bonds of worldly love, we are committed to practicing chastity and to helping others protect themselves. We are aware that loneliness and suffering cannot be alleviated by

the coming together of two bodies in a sexual relationship, but by the practice of true understanding and compassion. We know that a sexual relationship will destroy our life as a monk or a nun, will prevent us from realizing our ideal of serving living beings, and will harm others. We are determined not to suppress or mistreat our body or to look upon our body as only an instrument, but to learn to handle our body with respect. We are determined to preserve vital energies (sexual, breath, spirit) for the realization of our bodhisattva ideal.

(silence)

This is the Fourteenth Mindfulness Training of the Order of Interbeing. Have you studied, practiced, and observed it during the past two weeks?

(bell)

CONCLUDING WORDS

Brothers and Sisters, I have recited the Fourteen Mindfulness Trainings of the Order of Interbeing as the community has wished. I thank all my sisters and brothers for helping me do it serenely.

Please join your palms and recite each line of the closing chant after me:

> *Reciting the trainings,*
> *practicing the way of awareness,*
> *gives rise to benefits without limit.*
> *We vow to share the fruits with all beings.*
> *We vow to offer tribute to parents, teachers,*
> *friends, and numerous beings*
> *who give guidance and support along the path.*

4

TRANSMISSION OF THE FOURTEEN MINDFULNESS
TRAININGS OF THE ORDER OF INTERBEING

(The Fourteen Mindfulness Trainings can only be transmitted by a Dharma Teacher in the Order of Interbeing, assisted by three ordained members of the core community of the Order. All members of the Sangha, whether of the core or the extended community, are invited to attend.)

INCENSE OFFERING

In gratitude, we offer this incense to all Buddhas and bodhisattvas throughout space and time. May it be fragrant as Earth herself, reflecting our careful efforts, our wholehearted awareness, and the fruit of understanding, slowly ripening in us. May we and all beings be companions of Buddhas and bodhisattvas. May we awaken from forgetfulness and realize our true home.

(bell)

TOUCHING THE EARTH

Bringing light into the Ten Directions, the Buddha, the Dharma, and the Sangha, to whom we bow in gratitude.

(bell)

Teaching and living the way of awareness in the very midst of suffering and confusion, Shakyamuni Buddha, the Awakened One, to whom we bow in gratitude.

(bell)

Cutting through ignorance, awakening our hearts and minds, Manjushri, the Bodhisattva of Great Understanding, to whom we bow in gratitude.

(bell)

Working mindfully, working joyfully for the sake of all beings, Samantabhadra, the Bodhisattva of Great Action, to whom we bow in gratitude.

(bell)

Responding to suffering, serving beings in countless ways, Avalokiteshvara, the Bodhisattva of Great Compassion, to whom we bow in gratitude.

(bell)

Leading the Sangha, the ancestor Mahakashyapa, to whom we bow in gratitude.

(bell)

Wise elder brother, the teacher Shariputra, to whom we bow in gratitude.

(bell)

Showing love to his parents, Mahamaudgalyayana, to whom we bow in gratitude.

(bell)

Master of the Vinaya, the teacher Upali, to whom we bow in gratitude.

(bell)

Recording the teachings, the teacher Ananda, to whom we bow in gratitude.

(bell)

The first bhikshuni, Mahagotami, to whom we bow in gratitude.

(bell)

Showing the way fearlessly and compassionately, the stream
of ancestral teachers, to whom we bow in gratitude.

(two sounds of the bell)

OPENING CHANT

The Dharma is deep and lovely.
We now have a chance to see it,
study it, and practice it.
We vow to realize its true meaning.

THE HEART OF THE PRAJÑAPARAMITA

The Bodhisattva Avalokita,
While moving in the deep course of perfect understanding,
Shed light on the five skandhas
And found them equally empty.
After this penetration, he overcame ill-being.

(bell)

Listen, Shariputra,
Form is emptiness, emptiness is form.
Form is not other than emptiness.
Emptiness is not other than form.
The same is true with feelings,
Perceptions, mental formations, and consciousness.

(bell)

Hear, Shariputra,
All dharmas are marked with emptiness.
They are neither produced nor destroyed,
Neither defiled nor immaculate,
Neither increasing nor decreasing.

Therefore in emptiness there is neither form,
Nor feelings, nor perceptions,
Nor mental formations, nor consciousness;
No eye, or ear, or nose, or tongue, or body, or mind;
No form, no sound, no smell, no taste, no touch, no object
of mind;
No realms of elements (from eyes to mind consciousness);
No interdependent origins and no extinction of them
(From ignorance to death and decay);
No ill-being, no cause of ill-being,
No end of ill-being, and no path;
No understanding, no attainment.

(bell)

Because there is no attainment,
The bodhisattvas, grounded in perfect understanding,
Find no obstacles for their minds.
Having no obstacles, they overcome fear,
Liberating themselves forever from illusion
And realizing perfect nirvana.
All Buddhas in the past, present, and future,
Thanks to this perfect understanding,
Arrive at full, right, and universal enlightenment.

(bell)

Therefore one should know that perfect understanding
Is the highest mantra, the unequaled mantra,
The destroyer of ill-being, the incorruptible truth.
A mantra of prajñaparamita should therefore be pro-
claimed.

This is the mantra:

Gate gate paragate
Parasamgate
Bodhi Svaha.

(three sounds of the bell)

SANGHAKARMAN PROCEDURE

Sanghakarman Master: Has the whole community assembled?

Sanghakarman Convener: The whole community has assembled.

Sanghakarman Master: Is there harmony in the community?

Sanghakarman Convener: Yes, there is harmony.

Sanghakarman Master: Why has the community assembled?

Sanghakarman Convener: The community has assembled to perform the sanghakarman of transmitting the Fourteen Mindfulness Trainings of the Order of Interbeing.

Sanghakarman Master: Noble community of Interbeing, today,____(date)____, has been chosen as the day to transmit the Fourteen Mindfulness Trainings of the Order of Interbeing. The community has assembled at the appointed time and is ready to transmit and receive the Fourteen Mindfulness Trainings in an atmosphere of harmony. Thus, the transmission can proceed.

Is that correct?

Everyone: Correct.

(repeat question and answer three times)

BOWING IN GRATITUDE

In gratitude to their fathers and mothers who gave them birth, the ordinees bow deeply before the Three Jewels in the Ten Directions.

(bell)

In gratitude to their teachers who have shown them how to love, understand, and abide happily in the present moment, the ordinees bow deeply before the Three Jewels in the Ten Directions.

(bell)

In gratitude to friends who guide them on the path and offer support in difficult moments, the ordinees bow deeply before the Three Jewels in the Ten Directions.

(two sounds of the bell)

INTRODUCTORY WORDS

Today the community has gathered to give spiritual support to our brothers and sisters____(names)____ at the solemn moment when they will undertake to receive and observe the Mindfulness Trainings of the Order of Interbeing and enter the core community of the Order of Interbeing.

Ordinees, please listen. Following in the steps of the bodhisattvas as your teachers and companions on the path, you have made the aspiration to receive and observe the Mindfulness Trainings of the Order of Interbeing. You have given rise to the seed of *bodhichitta*, the mind of love. You have made it your aspiration to develop this seed. Your own awakening and liberation, as well as the liberation and awakening of all other species, have now become your highest career. Brothers and Sisters in the community, please establish your mindfulness by enjoying your breathing, so that you may be truly present and give support to the seed of the mind of love in the ordinees. With your support, they will develop this seed solidly and courageously so that it will become indestructible.

Ordinees, this is a solemn moment for receiving the Fourteen Mindfulness Trainings of the Order of Interbeing. Listen carefully, with a clear and concentrated mind, to each mindfulness training as it is read, and answer, "Yes, I do," clearly every time you see that you have the intention and capacity to receive, learn about, and practice the mindfulness training that has been read.

(bell)

Ordinees, are you ready?

Ordinees: Yes, I am.

THE FOURTEEN MINDFULNESS TRAININGS

These then are the Fourteen Mindfulness Trainings of the Order of Interbeing.

THE FIRST MINDFULNESS TRAINING

Aware of the suffering created by fanaticism and intolerance, we are determined not to be idolatrous about or bound to any doctrine, theory, or ideology, even Buddhist ones. Buddhist teachings are guiding means to help us learn to look deeply and to develop our understanding and compassion. They are not doctrines to fight, kill, or die for.

(silence)

This is the First Mindfulness Training of the Order of Inter-being. Do you make the commitment to receive, learn about, and practice it in your daily life?

Ordinees: Yes, I do.

(bell)

THE SECOND MINDFULNESS TRAINING

Aware of the suffering created by attachment to views and wrong perceptions, we are determined to avoid being narrow-minded and bound to present views. We shall learn and practice nonattachment from views in order to be open to others' insights and experiences. We are aware that the knowledge we presently possess is not changeless, absolute truth. Truth is found in life, and we will observe life within and around us in every moment, ready to learn throughout our lives.

(silence)

This is the Second Mindfulness Training of the Order of Interbeing. Do you make the commitment to receive, learn about, and practice it in your daily life?

Ordinees: Yes, I do.

(bell)

THE THIRD MINDFULNESS TRAINING

Aware of the suffering brought about when we impose our views on others, we are committed not to force others, even our children, by any means whatsoever—such as authority, threat, money, propaganda, or indoctrination—to adopt our views. We will respect the right of others to be different and to choose what to believe and how to decide. We will, however, help others renounce fanaticism and narrowness through compassionate dialogue.

(silence)

This is the Third Mindfulness Training of the Order of Interbeing. Do you make the commitment to receive, learn about, and practice it in your daily life?

Ordinees: Yes, I do.

(bell)

THE FOURTH MINDFULNESS TRAINING

Aware that looking deeply at the nature of suffering can help us develop compassion and find ways out of suffering, we are determined not to avoid or close our eyes before suffering. We are committed to finding ways, including personal contact, images, and sounds, to be with those who suffer, so we can understand their situation deeply and help them transform their suffering into compassion, peace, and joy.

(silence)

This is the Fourth Mindfulness Training of the Order of Interbeing. Do you make the commitment to receive, learn about, and practice it in your daily life?

Ordinees: Yes, I do.

(bell)

THE FIFTH MINDFULNESS TRAINING

Aware that true happiness is rooted in peace, solidity, freedom, and compassion, and not in wealth or fame, we are determined not to take as the aim of our life fame, profit, wealth, or sensual pleasure, nor to accumulate wealth while millions are hungry and dying. We are committed to living simply and sharing our time, energy, and material resources with those in need. We will practice mindful consuming, not using alcohol, drugs, or any other products that bring toxins into our own and the collective body and consciousness.

(silence)

This is the Fifth Mindfulness Training of the Order of Interbeing. Do you make the commitment to receive, learn about, and practice it in your daily life?

Ordinees: Yes, I do.

(bell)

THE SIXTH MINDFULNESS TRAINING

Aware that anger blocks communication and creates suffering, we are determined to take care of the energy of anger when it arises and to recognize and transform the seeds of anger that lie deep in our consciousness. When anger comes up, we are determined not to do or say anything, but to practice mindful breathing or mindful walking and acknowledge, embrace, and look deeply into our anger. We will learn to look with the eyes of compassion at those we think are the cause of our anger.

(silence)

This is the Sixth Mindfulness Training of the Order of Interbeing. Do you make the commitment to receive, learn about, and practice it in your daily life?

Ordinees: Yes, I do.

(bell)

THE SEVENTH MINDFULNESS TRAINING

Aware that life is available only in the present moment and that it is possible to live happily in the here and now, we are committed to training ourselves to live deeply each moment of daily life. We will try not to lose ourselves in dispersion or be carried away by regrets about the past, worries about the future, or craving, anger, or jealousy in the present. We will practice mindful breathing to come back to what is happening in the present moment. We are determined to learn the art of mindful living by touching the wondrous, refreshing, and healing elements that are inside and around us, and by nourishing seeds of joy, peace, love, and understanding in ourselves, thus facilitating the work of transformation and healing in our consciousness.

(silence)

This is the Seventh Mindfulness Training of the Order of Interbeing. Do you make the commitment to receive, learn about, and practice it in your daily life?

Ordinees: Yes, I do.

(bell)

THE EIGHTH MINDFULNESS TRAINING

Aware that the lack of communication always brings separation and suffering, we are committed to training ourselves in the practice of compassionate listening and loving speech. We will learn to listen deeply without judging or reacting and refrain from uttering words that can create discord or cause the community to break. We will make every effort to keep communications open and to reconcile and resolve all conflicts, however small.

(silence)

This is the Eighth Mindfulness Training of the Order of Interbeing. Do you make the commitment to receive, learn about, and practice it in your daily life?

Ordinees: Yes, I do.

(bell)

THE NINTH MINDFULNESS TRAINING

Aware that words can create suffering or happiness, we are committed to learning to speak truthfully and constructively, using only words that inspire hope and confidence. We are determined not to say untruthful things for the sake of personal interest or to impress people, nor to utter words that might cause division or hatred. We will not spread news that we do not know to be certain nor criticize or condemn things of which we are not sure. We will do our best to speak out about situations of injustice, even when doing so may threaten our safety.

(silence)

This is the Ninth Mindfulness Training of the Order of Interbeing. Do you make the commitment to receive, learn about, and practice it in your daily life?

Ordinees: Yes, I do.

(bell)

THE TENTH MINDFULNESS TRAINING

Aware that the essence and aim of a Sangha is the practice of understanding and compassion, we are determined not to use the Buddhist community for personal gain or profit or transform our community into a political instrument. A spiritual community should, however, take a clear stand against oppression and injustice and should strive to change the situation without engaging in partisan conflicts.

(silence)

This is the Tenth Mindfulness Training of the Order of Interbeing. Do you make the commitment to receive, learn about, and practice it in your daily life?

Ordinees: Yes, I do.

(bell)

THE ELEVENTH MINDFULNESS TRAINING

Aware that great violence and injustice have been done to our environment and society, we are committed not to live with a vocation that is harmful to humans and nature. We will do our best to select a livelihood that helps realize our ideal of understanding and compassion. Aware of global economic, political and social realities, we will behave responsibly as consumers and as citizens, not investing in companies that deprive others of their chance to live.

(silence)

This is the Eleventh Mindfulness Training of the Order of Interbeing. Do you make the commitment to receive, learn about, and practice it in your daily life?

Ordinees: Yes, I do.

(bell)

THE TWELFTH MINDFULNESS TRAINING

Aware that much suffering is caused by war and conflict, we are determined to cultivate nonviolence, understanding, and compassion in our daily lives, to promote peace education, mindful mediation, and reconciliation within families, communities, nations, and in the world. We are determined not to kill and not to let others kill. We will diligently practice deep looking with our Sangha to discover better ways to protect life and prevent war.

(silence)

This is the Twelfth Mindfulness Training of the Order of Interbeing. Do you make the commitment to receive, learn about, and practice it in your daily life?

Ordinees: Yes, I do.

(bell)

THE THIRTEENTH MINDFULNESS TRAINING

Aware of the suffering caused by exploitation, social injustice, stealing, and oppression, we are committed to cultivating loving kindness and learning ways to work for the well-being of people, animals, plants, and minerals. We will practice generosity by sharing our time, energy, and material resources with those who are in need. We are determined not to steal and not to possess anything that should belong to others. We will respect the property of others, but will try to prevent others from profiting from human suffering or the suffering of other beings.

(silence)

This is the Thirteenth Mindfulness Training of the Order of Interbeing. Do you make the commitment to receive, learn about, and practice it in your daily life?

Ordinees: Yes, I do.

(bell)

THE FOURTEENTH MINDFULNESS TRAINING

(For lay members): Aware that sexual relations motivated by craving cannot dissipate the feeling of loneliness but will create more suffering, frustration, and isolation, we are determined not to engage in sexual relations without mutual understanding, love, and a long-term commitment. In sexual relations, we must be aware of future suffering that may be caused. We know that to preserve the happiness of ourselves and others, we must respect the rights and commitments of ourselves and others. We will do everything in our power to protect children from sexual abuse and to protect couples and families from being broken by sexual misconduct. We will treat our bodies with respect and preserve our vital energies (sexual, breath, spirit) for the realization of our bodhisattva ideal. We will be fully aware of the responsibility of bringing new lives into the world, and will meditate on the world into which we are bringing new beings.

(For monastic members): Aware that the aspiration of a monk or a nun can only be realized when he or she wholly leaves behind the bonds of worldly love, we are committed to practicing chastity and to helping others protect themselves. We are aware that loneliness and suffering cannot be alleviated by

the coming together of two bodies in a sexual relationship, but by the practice of true understanding and compassion. We know that a sexual relationship will destroy our life as a monk or a nun, will prevent us from realizing our ideal of serving living beings, and will harm others. We are determined not to suppress or mistreat our body or to look upon our body as only an instrument, but to learn to handle our body with respect. We are determined to preserve vital energies (sexual, breath, spirit) for the realization of our bodhisattva ideal.

(silence)

This is the Fourteenth Mindfulness Training of the Order of Interbeing. Do you make the commitment to receive, learn about, and practice it in your daily life?

Ordinees: Yes, I do.

(bell)

CONCLUDING WORDS

Ordinees, you have received the Fourteen Mindfulness Trainings of the Order of Interbeing. You have taken the first step on the path of the bodhisattvas: the path of great understanding of Bodhisattva Manjushri that puts an end to countless wrong perceptions, prejudice, and discrimination; the path of great compassion of Bodhisattva Avalokiteshvara, who loves, values, and protects the life of all species and listens deeply to the cries of all species far and near in order to help them; the path of great action of Bodhisattva Samantabhadra, who takes every opportunity to create love, understanding, and harmony in the world.

Brothers and Sisters in the community, with one heart please give your spiritual support to the ordinees in this present moment to help them now and in the future. Brothers and Sisters, the Buddhas and bodhisattvas will be with you on your path of practice. When you hear the sound of the bell, please stand up and bow deeply three times to show your gratitude to the Three Jewels. Noble community, please concentrate your mind in order to recite the name of the Buddha so that the mindfulness trainings body of the ordinees may be courageous and strong and endure.

RECITING THE BUDDHA'S NAME

Namo Shakyamunaya Buddhaya

(repeat each name three times)

Namo Manjushraya Bodhisattvaya
Namo Samantabhadraya Bodhisattvaya
Namo Avalokitaya Bodhisattvaya

TRANSMISSION OF CERTIFICATE OF ORDINATION AND BROWN JACKET (IF AVAILABLE)

THE THREE JEWELS

I take refuge in the Buddha,
the one who shows me the way in this life.
Namo Buddhaya.

I take refuge in the Dharma,
the way of understanding and love.
Namo Dharmaya.

I take refuge in the Sangha,
the community that lives in harmony and awareness.
Namo Sanghaya.

Buddham saranam gacchami.
Dharmam saranam gacchami.
Sangham saranam gacchami.

CLOSING CHANT

Please join your palms and recite each line of the closing
chant after me:

Reciting the trainings,
practicing the way of awareness,
gives rise to benefits without limit.
We vow to share the fruits with all beings.
We vow to offer tribute to parents, teachers,
friends, and numerous beings
who give guidance and support along the path.

PART FOUR

The Charter of the Order of Interbeing

The Charter of the Order of Interbeing
(Tiep Hien)

CHAPTER I
NAME, AIM, TRADITION

1. A Buddhist community is formed with the name Order of Interbeing.

2. The aim of the Order is to actualize Buddhism by studying, experimenting with, and applying Buddhism in modern life with a special emphasis on the bodhisattva ideal.

3. The Order of Interbeing was founded within the Linji School of Dhyana Buddhism. It is grounded in the Four Spirits: the spirit of nonattachment from views, the spirit of direct experimentation on the nature of interdependent origination through meditation, the spirit of appropriateness, and the spirit of skillful means. All four are to be found in all Buddhist traditions.

CHAPTER II
BASIC SCRIPTURES, TEACHINGS, METHODS

4. The Order of Interbeing does not consider any sutra or group of sutras as its basic scripture(s). It draws inspiration from the essence of the Buddhadharma in all sutras. It does not accept the systematic arrangements of the Buddhist teachings proposed by any school. The Order of Interbeing seeks to realize the spirit of the Dharma in early Buddhism, as well as in the development of that spirit through the history of the Sangha, and its life and teachings in all Buddhist traditions.

5. The Order of Interbeing considers all sutras, whether spoken by the Lord Buddha or compiled by later Buddhist generations, as Buddhist sutras. It is also able to find inspiration from the texts of other spiritual traditions. It considers the development of original Buddhism into new schools a necessity to keep the spirit of Buddhism alive. Only by proposing new forms of Buddhist life can one help the true Buddhist spirit perpetuate.

6. The life of the Order of Interbeing should be nourished by understanding and compassion. Compassion and understanding, radiated by the Buddhist life, can contribute to the peace and happiness of humankind. The Order considers the principle of nonattachment from views and the principle of direct experimentation on interdependent origination through meditation to be the two most important guides for attaining true understanding. It considers the principle of appropriateness and the principle of skillful means as guides for actions in society. The spirit of nonattachment from views and the spirit of direct experimentation lead to open-mindedness and compassion, both in the realm of the perception of reality and in the realm of human relationships. The spirit of appropriateness and the spirit of skillful means lead to a capacity to be creative and to reconcile, both of which are necessary for the service of living beings.

7. The Order of Interbeing rejects dogmatism in both looking and acting. It seeks all forms of action that can revive and sustain the true spirit of insight and compassion in life. It considers this spirit to be more important than any Buddhist institution or tradition. With the aspiration of a

bodhisattva, members of the Order of Interbeing seek to change themselves in order to change society in the direction of compassion and understanding by living a joyful and mindful life.

CHAPTER III
AUTHORITY, MEMBERSHIP, ORGANIZATION

8. To protect and respect the freedom and responsibility of each member of the community, monks, nuns, and laypeople enjoy equality in the Order of Interbeing.

9. The Order of Interbeing does not recognize the necessity of a mediator between the Buddha and lay disciples, between humans and ultimate reality. It considers, however, the insight and experiences of ancestral teachers, monks, nuns, and laypeople, as helpful to those who are practicing the Way.

10. Members of the Order of Interbeing are either in the core community or the extended community. The core community consists of those who have made the commitment to observe the Fourteen Mindfulness Trainings of the Order and the Five Mindfulness Trainings, and who have been ordained as brothers and sisters in the Order. The extended community consists of members who, while trying to live the spirit of the Order of Interbeing, have not formally made the commitment to observe the Fourteen Mindfulness Trainings, nor received ordination in the Order of Interbeing. The members of the core community accept the responsibility to organize and support a local Sangha, and help sustain mindfulness training recitations, days of mindfulness, and mindfulness retreats.

11. The extended community lives in close relationship with the core community by attending the recitation of the mindfulness trainings every two weeks and by participating in spiritual and social events sponsored by the core community. Long-standing members of the extended community, those who have participated regularly for one year or more, should be consulted on an advisory basis on the applications of individuals to become members of the core community, whether or not these long-standing members of the extended community have received the Five Mindfulness Trainings.

12. *Dharmacharyas* (Dharma Teachers) are members of the core community who have been selected as teachers based on their stability in the practice and ability to lead a happy life. They function to inspire joy and stability in the local Sanghas. Local Sanghas are encouraged to suggest potential Dharmacharyas.

CHAPTER IV
MINDFULNESS TRAININGS OF THE ORDER OF INTERBEING,
CONDITIONS FOR ORDINATION

13. The mindfulness trainings of the Order of Interbeing reflect the life of the Order, which considers spiritual practice as the base of all social action.

14. The mindfulness trainings are the heart of the Charter. Members are expected to recite the Five Mindfulness Trainings and the Fourteen Mindfulness Trainings every two weeks. If there is a three-month lapse in their recitation, their ordination is considered nullified.

15. All persons eighteen years old or older, regardless of race, nationality, color, gender, or sexual orientation, are eligible to join the Order if they have shown the capacity of learning and practicing the Mindfulness Trainings and other requirements of a core community member of the Order of Interbeing, and have formally received the Three Jewels and the Five Mindfulness Trainings.

16. A candidate begins the application process by announcing his or her aspiration to become a member of the core community of the Order of Interbeing. The announcement should be in writing to the local Sangha core community members, or if none are located nearby, to the appropriate Dharma Teacher(s). A candidate must have received the Three Jewels and Five Mindfulness Trainings. One or more core community members shall then mentor and train the candidate for at least one year, until the candidate is happy and steadfast in the practice and practices in harmony with the Sangha. These steps enable the aspirant to get to know the core community better. Similarly, they enable the core community to get to know the aspirant better, to offer guidance and support, especially in areas of the practice where the aspirant may need additional guidance, and to train the aspirant in the role of Order member. When appropriate, the core community members and Dharma Teacher(s) will decide, after making an advisory consultation with long-standing members of the extended community, whether or not that candidate is ready to receive ordination into the Order of Interbeing. The work of a core community Order member includes Sangha building and support, explaining the Dharma from personal experience, and nourishing the bodhichitta in others while maintaining

a regular meditation practice in harmony and peace with one's family, all as manifestations of the bodhisattva ideal.

17. When the core community and the Dharma Teacher(s) make a decision on an application, they will strive to use their Sangha eyes and take care to nourish the bodhichitta of the aspirant, even if a delay in ordination is suggested. Local Sanghas are authorized to embellish the application procedures in this Charter in a manner that reasonably addresses local culture, geography, and circumstances, provided that the goals and aspirations of the Order are not defeated. The application provisions set forth in the Charter respecting an individual's ordination may be waived in individual cases under special circumstances such as medical hardship, provided that, as appropriate, the coordinators of the Executive Council and most appropriate Dharma Teacher(s) are consulted first, and, if time permits, the local or most appropriate core community members. When it has been indicated that the candidate is ready to receive the Order ordination, his or her name shall be reported to the person designated by the core community Assembly. When an ordination ceremony has taken place, it shall be declared in writing to the Secretary of the Order, giving the name, lineage name, and Dharma name of the ordinee; date and place of the ordination; and the name of the presiding Dharma Teacher.

18. Members of the core community are expected to observe at least sixty days of mindfulness per year. It is recognized that this sixty-day requirement may be difficult for some members to achieve at times, due to family or other re-

sponsibilities, and the requirement is intended to be flexible in such cases, if it is agreed upon by the Sangha.

19. All members of the core community are expected to organize and practice with a local Sangha.

20. Provided they are consistent with the spirit of the Five Mindfulness Trainings and the Fourteen Mindfulness Trainings, all lifestyles (whether in a committed relationship or celibate) are considered equally valid for core community members. To support both partners in a relationship, it is helpful if the partner of a core community member is a member of the core community, a member of the extended community, or, at the minimum, that the member live in harmony with his or her partner and that the member's partner supports and encourages the member's practice.

CHAPTER V
LEADERSHIP, COMMUNITY PROPERTIES, ACCOUNTING

21. At regular intervals, an Assembly of all core community members should gather for a council. All members shall be notified six months in advance of the date and location of the meeting. Any member unable to attend can appoint a proxy to speak for him or her. The process of consensus shall be presented, reviewed, and revised at the beginning of the meeting. Rotating teams of facilitators, one woman and one man, each of different nationality, shall conduct the meeting. Minutes of each meeting of the Assembly will be kept as an ongoing record of the life and work of the Order of Interbeing. They will be made available to members on request.

22. At the Assembly meeting, the core community will select members to serve on an Executive Council to organize
and guide the work of the Order of Interbeing between As-
semblies, and to approve coordinators of the Executive
Council from among the members of the Executive Council. The Assembly will decide on the specific structure and
organization that will best support the goals of reducing suffering, realizing the bodhisattva ideal, and maintaining a
strong Sangha network. The core community will draw on
the life maturity and practice maturity of its elders and on
the freshness of its younger members for assistance and support, and encourage and benefit from an ongoing Council
of Elders and Council of Youth.

23. In order to facilitate interaction with the worldwide
Sangha, local Sanghas are encouraged to organize in a manner compatible with the spirit of this Charter.

24. To be a member of the Order core community one is
not required to pay financial dues, but dues may be suggested by the Executive Council and the Assembly as *dana*
(donation) to support the work of the Order. All Order of
Interbeing monies, including contributions and dues, are to
be held in a separate fund under the name "Order of
Interbeing." A detailed financial report prepared by the
Treasurer(s) shall be presented to the membership annually.
After administrative costs have been covered, funds of the
Order may be used to help local Sanghas offer scholarships
to members to attend Order retreats and in their work to re-
lieve suffering.

25. Any community properties of the Order should be held under the national and local regulations of its site. To protect those who may be responsible for the management of community properties, all assets, including bank accounts, currency, real estate, vehicles, etc., are to be accounted for using common accounting practices. If and when local Sanghas hold funds for the international Order of Interbeing, accounting will be kept separately and detailed reports sent yearly to the Treasurer(s) of the Order.

CHAPTER VI
AMENDMENT OF THE CHARTER

26. Every word and every sentence in this Charter is subject to change, so that the spirit of the Charter will be allowed to remain alive throughout the history of the practice. Previous versions should be preserved and made available for consultation by later generations. All versions are to be clearly dated for future reference.

27. The Fourteen Mindfulness Trainings and this Charter are to be reexamined at each Assembly of the core community members.

28. This Charter, consisting of six chapters and twenty-nine items should be revised and amended at each Assembly of the core community members in order to keep it relevant to today's societies.

29. In keeping with the tradition of the Sangha, all changes must be made by consensus and not just by simple majority.

Plum Village is a retreat community in southwestern France where monks, nuns, laymen, and laywomen practice the art of mindful living. Visitors are invited to join the practice for at least one week. For information about Plum Village, please contact:

PlumVillage
13 Martineau
33580 Dieulivol
France

For more information about the Order of Interbeing, please contact Plum Village or the Community of Mindful Living.

Parallax Press publishes books and tapes on Buddhism and related subjects to make them accessible and alive for contemporary readers. It is our hope that doing so will help alleviate suffering and create a more peaceful world. We carry all books and tapes by Thich Nhat Hanh. For a copy of our free catalog, please write:

Community of Mindful Living / Parallax Press
P.O. Box 7355
Berkeley, California 94707
www.parallax.org